Lessons from the Water

Lessons from the Water

a Swimmer's Journey through the Tides of Life

Katie Blair

ISBN-13: 9798674807315

Dedication

To my son Ashton, some days I am not sure who raised whom. Follow your passion, you already know where you are going. To Muschka, my North Star and kindred spirit. To my parents, Annette and Jürgen, for always doing the very best they could and for always being there for Ashton and I.

Table of Contents

Foreword

Many people write books, and I was concerned whether I had enough to say to make a contribution, or if it would be conceited or self-indulgent to make it all about me. Now in my 40s, at a new juncture in life that has brought an unimaginable peace and comfort within myself, I am thinking maybe – just maybe – there is some type of wisdom to be gained from my wildly unusual, impulsive, and adventurous life. You will be the judge as to how useful my shared adventures may be to you, but never doubt that we all are the experts of our own lives who must be the relentless, beautiful heroes of our own stories.

My grandmother, who left me with so many sayings that still echo in my mind and soul, used to say (in German): "First, it will be different. Second, it will be different from what you think it will be." I find this simple statement to be one of the very few fundamental truths of life I have encountered. This book is also dedicated to her because, without her, my story would have been quite different. To this day, years after her death, I still hear her voice from when she used to call me from Germany: "Child, are you still swimming?" Yes, the child is still swimming – not to be in great competitions, not for records, medals, or any other extrinsic reward, but because swimming is what I do.

Chapter 1

Lessons from the Bottom of the Swimming Pool

While many words were used to describe me as a child, none of them were particularly flattering or in any way suggested normalcy. My mother, a hardworking high school teacher of German and French, taught at the school she once attended and eventually retired from. My father worked for Lufthansa airlines as a systems analyst for his entire career. Neither left my hometown of Mannheim, Germany, for anything else but the occasional nice vacation. They worked hard, and my maternal grandmother (nicknamed "Muschka" by her husband) prevented me from being another '80s latchkey kid. My earliest memories are getting in trouble in kindergarten for running too much, being too wild, fighting too much and generally not really being a "good little girl." I remember adults always wanting me to sleep; instead, I sneaked around dark apartments wondering why they were all sleeping so much. My energy was boundless, and so was my curiosity, my desire for justice, and the depth of my little thoughts.

I must have been about 4 years old and sleeping in my grandmother's apartment when I suddenly awoke at night to the most terrifying thought I had had in my tiny existence: My little life would be finite, and so would the time Muschka and I had together in this apartment, where I felt so safe and loved. Hysterically crying, I woke her up to explain to her my urgent insight that she would likely die first, that I would be lost in a world without her and proclaimed that she was not allowed to die before me. Gently, she comforted me and told me she would most certainly not die while I still needed her, but that there would be a day when I would be an adult and I would no longer need her (which sent me into more hysterical crying). I remember demanding a certain specific date or number of years and coming up with the number 32. I am not quite sure, but I think I arrived at that number by guesstimating human life expectancy. When I would reach age 32, my grandmother would be 88 – a ripe, old age. Muschka did not actually leave me until 2015, when I was almost 37, but given her stubbornness her word was not to be broken.

You may wonder if I grew up reading Jean Paul Sartre, wearing black turtlenecks and calling myself an existentialist, but despite my early struggles, I went quite a different route in my search for meaning. (Speaking of which, if in your entire existence, you only read one book, immediately discard this book, and obtain a copy of Holocaust survivor and psychiatrist Viktor Frankl's book *Man's Search for Meaning*. It is by far the most powerful testimony to the resilience of the human spirit you will ever read. But I am digressing, as I do often in life).

My childhood nickname was "Kathi," and Kathi was in trouble often. In elementary school, my grandmother was a regular at the principal's office to discuss either my unusually and poorly-timed outspoken nature or for physical fighting, both of which quickly earned me the intriguing label "behaviorally disturbed." I mainly remember the tedious, repetitive mind-numbing lessons and the torture of sitting still. You may think I was underchallenged, which I certainly was, but the issue was much deeper than that, and I could feel it. I was fundamentally different and saw the world differently. Other 6 year-olds did not find Barbie offensive, but I remember being outraged at the idea I would one day be sitting in the hair salon to get my hair curled, and the best part of my Barbie days would be walking my puppy and having fancy dinners with Ken. I generally got along better with little boys, as I loved moving around and exploring. My BMX bike was my heart and soul. Muschka bought me a little watch so I could report in on the hour.

So, I knew early on that I was different – "wild with a good heart" as my grandmother tried to explain to the teachers and principal. I was about 6 when my well-intentioned parents signed me up for tennis class during a vacation in Switzerland, but all I could think of was the heat and my annoyance with what appeared to be a senseless and redundant cycle of hitting the balls and picking them up.

One day I realized the place at the resort that truly had my heart was the swimming pool. It took everybody a little to find me, but when they did, I had been somersaulting at the bottom of the pool for quite some time, occasionally bobbing up to the surface to deal with the inconvenience of breathing. I looked up through the water at the people walking by with ice cream. They were blurry, distant and inaudible. My burning desire was to stay at the bottom of the pool, at a safe and blurry distance from a world I found quite cruel and confusing.

Wild with a good heart, and always curious.

Unsurprisingly, my first sentence in the English language was "Do you have a swimming pool?" and, starting at age 7, I asked this same question of every single hotel receptionist we encountered during our trips to the U.S. I remembered destinations, not the way others did, but by how the water felt. I remember American pools being heavily chlorinated, warm and shallow. I would spend every waking minute of our vacations in the tiny swimming pool, enjoying the weightlessness and the feeling of floating.

Standing still and constrictive dresses. Misery.

Even though my love for water came early and instantaneously, competitive swimming, for some odd reason, was not really a consideration until later. Muschka started me on ballet classes at age 4, and by age 10, I joined the State Academy of Dance in Mannheim with the fierce dream of becoming a dancer. The school was rigorous and my work ethic exceptional. If it was doable, trainable and practicable, I would get it done.

While I progressed well as a dancer, I also grew taller each year, and finally, at age 13, I was given the world-shattering news that I would not be allowed to return the next year. I had been concerned over my height for some time and desperately tried to starve myself to prevent myself from growing – a misguided attempt that left me with an uncomfortable relationship with my own body, which I thought had betrayed me, as well as food itself, which had ceased to be just nutrition but was now a battleground on which to test my willpower and control.

Many tears and a failed attempt at gymnastics later, (I still consider gymnastics the king of all sports, by the way), I finally decided I would give synchronized swimming a try. The day I went to my first practice, I learned there no longer was a synchronized swimming team in the area due to lack of interest, but I would be welcome to swim with the preparatory swim team of 8- to 10-year-olds.

I still remember the feeling of not being able to breathe. I struggled fiercely behind the slowest child in the slowest lane. Disoriented, I swallowed water and felt it burning and stinging my nose as I struggled to get from one side of the pool to the other. I was shocked. I thought myself a good dancer and athlete, but I could barely breathe, and I was truly upset at myself. The instructor was kind and encouraged me to return, but she didn't need to. My mind had already been made up: I would learn how to swim, no matter what it took. I would be able to glide from one side of the pool to the other.

The preparatory team only trained twice a week, but on the other days, I rode my bike to the public swimming pool. And I practiced. A lot. Slowly but surely, I moved to the faster lanes. One day, a coach from the main swim team watched our practice and invited me to swim with "the real team." I was ecstatic.

With my parents considering my dance and now my swimming a waste of time and my Muschka never having had a driver's license, I would rely on public transportation to get to and from practice. The first few months were not very glorious. I was once again at the back of the slow lane and at times, I even had my own lane, as I was unable to keep up with swimmers who had trained since they were 4. I was now 14, and for swimming, that is a ridiculously late start. More than one of the girls asked me why I was even trying.

But something happened. I still loved the water and the breathing got a little easier – particularly when I used the backstroke, which aided my breathing. I could feel my progress. I didn't focus on my parents telling me I was wasting my time or the other swimmers looking down on me; I just focused on the water. The coach saw something in me as well. Call it intrinsic motivation, mindset, drive, or a never-quit attitude, I was hardheaded and failure-resistant. I *really* wanted to be a swimmer.

And then one day, about a year later, I was warming up in some of the "regular speed" lanes at a local swim meet. Now, many of the other swimmers were accompanied by their parents, who meticulously monitored not only their own children's progress, but also their competitors, as they vicariously lived through their young hopefuls. I swam the starting leg of the 4 x 100-meter freestyle relay, as I had added freestyle to my repertoire. And I was fast.

An argument ensued after our relay. One parent argued her daughter, the second swimmer in the relay, had been wronged by a timing mistake that misrepresented her performance. These were the days of handheld stopwatches, and it was easy to believe I had benefitted from the error. There was no way I swam that fast.

About an hour later, feeling slightly unwelcome and wishing I, too, had a parent there, I stepped on the block for the 100-meter freestyle. I never once looked at anyone. I was breathing to the right every four strokes, focusing on long pulls and my fast kick. When I climbed out of the pool, I learned I had swum even faster than in the relay.

I ended up receiving a trophy for the best performance at the meet, and I walked around in a happy, confused haze. The same parent from earlier was talking to her daughter about how unfair it all was when I walked into the locker room with my little trophy. I quietly packed my swim bag and left. I had never, ever won a trophy before, and I kept it for almost 20 years, until it felt like it was finally time to let it go.

Training days in Germany.

From that day on, I was a regular member of the swim team. Respected by the coach and most of the team members, I was a real swimmer and it had become a normal part of my life, much like eating and sleeping. The time spent in the slow lane taught me more than many of my more glorious days. I learned to keep my head down, to have faith that consistency would get me where I wanted to be, and to dream even if my dreams made sense to no one else. These lessons went beyond sports, and they have been invaluable in navigating the wild and crazy ocean life can be.

Chapter 2

Lessons from the World's Biggest Washing Machine

And so, I had become a regular swimmer, hair like straw and always faintly smelling of chlorine. It was not uncommon to hear a classmate say "Man, I don't know what it is, but it smells like a jacuzzi in here." My life had become a solid routine of schoolwork and after-school practice and weekend swim meets. The same coach that had encouraged me early on now dedicated a lot of time to working with me one-on-one and driving me to swim meets all across the country. I was about 16, when one evening, I noticed a small group of athletes come into the pool after our practice ended. They were all a little older, and while they looked terribly fit and tan, their swimming technique left room for improvement. Eventually, I struck up a conversation with a particularly handsome young athlete named Alex, the group's only fast swimmer. He explained to me that he was a triathlete and had just returned from the Ironman Hawaii to do a little bit of off-season training.

This was 1994, and neither smartphones nor google were part of our world yet, so my only options to learn more were checking out some local library books and purchasing a copy of Triathlete magazine at the Mannheim train station. And you guessed it, I quickly became obsessed. These athletes were swimming 2.4 miles, biking 112 miles and running 26.2 miles – all back-to-back in the heat of Hawaii. It did not seem feasible for me, given I had never really ridden a race bike, and my only memories of running were dreadful physical education lessons in school. But because it seemed so impossible for a girl like me, I was even more intrigued. Soon, pictures of six-time Ironman Hawaii champ Paula Newby-Fraser (known as "The Queen of Kona" for the Hawaiian city that hosts the championship), graced my walls as I tried to find ways to get started. I began to stay after swim practice to add some mileage and hopefully snatch a ride home with Alex, who was 10 years my senior and lived in my part of town. On these drives, I learned how he got into the sport, what local events were available and what type of bike I should buy. Sponsored by my parents, I got a heavy steel-frame bike and quietly began biking and running.

During the next couple of years, I got my feet wet at some local triathlons and quickly earned the nickname "the swimmer," mainly because I was the only one without a wetsuit and typically got out of the water with a little bit of a lead. I was quite the natural on the bike, except for the mountains, where a tall girl like me paid a price for weighing significantly more than the shorter girls. Running was dreadful, a constant fight against gravity, heat, and my own body. I always felt hunted as my lead would shrink with every kilometer I ran.

My swim coach followed me to the triathlon world, and I was beginning to make a name for myself, eventually drawing some interest from the Junior National team. As that interest grew, so did the number of people wanting to have a say in my training and races. The performance pressure began to eat me alive.

My home team coach was less and less part of my journey as other coaches came into my life. Shortly after I turned 18, I began a romantic relationship with Alex, who had occasional advice but overall was pretty hands-off in my practice and training. Eventually, I ended up working with his coach, a well-known and highly successful Polish coach who had coached some of the fastest running triathletes in the world. I still remember the benign sentence that would set off a chain of events that would literally weigh on my life and my relationship with food and my own body forever. Desperate to fix my running problem, the Polish coach advised, "With every kilogram you lose, you should be able to run one minute faster in the 10K."

I began to restrict my food intake, and 6-hour bike rides on nothing but an apple became normal. After several months of doing this kind of thing, I arrived at home from a long bike ride, famished. I was so hungry I ran into my apartment and ate whatever was not tied down. That naturally resulted in me getting terribly nauseated, and I got sick. Part of me was hugely relieved that all these calories did not stick, but it started a dark cycle of restricting and binging and purging. No one knew my dark secret; they only saw my performance increasing. In 2000, I tackled my first Ironman in Panama City, Florida at age 21. I broke 11 hours, not bad for a kid. I ran dreadfully slow but did qualify for the Ironman Hawaii in the 18-24 age group.

ITU age-group world championship 2000.

In the summer of 2001, I had what I still consider my best Ironman race at the International Triathlon Union World Championship in Fredericia,

Denmark, where I won the 18-24 age group in 10 hours and 59 minutes – despite losing all but a few minutes of my one-hour lead during a dreadful run. My relationship with Alex became rocky as our race calendars took us to different places, and he started new relationships on the side. Meanwhile, after the Denmark race, I was in such bad shape from dehydration that I earned myself a spot in the medical tent, where I received some fluids. Next to me was a stunning Italian athlete whom I already had met at our hotel. We talked a little, and he invited me to race for his small local team in Verbania, Italy.

A dreadful run and a rainy finish in Fredericia, Denmark.

Shortly thereafter, my little Opel Corsa packed to the brim, I made the 6-hour drive to Italy, where I lived and trained in preparation for the Ironman Hawaii in October. One day, I came home from a long bike ride and started making lunch in the kitchen while flipping through the TV channels. It seemed like the same stupid movie was on every Italian station until I realized this was a news report. It was an eerie feeling as it finally dawned on me that someone had attacked the Americans. The Americans, who most countries view as invincible! Certainly, this meant if someone attacked Americans so boldly, no one was safe. The piazza in Italy was quiet that night as we ate our dinner. The mood was subdued, and the World Triathlon Cooperation (WTC) debated cancelling the Ironman Triathlon World Championship in Kona.

In the end, the WTC decided the race would take place and I took the 28-hour trip from Frankfurt, Germany, to Kona, Hawaii, where nerves were raw. The small town was overrun with 1,500 of the world's best triathletes and their entourages, and everywhere you looked someone was either swimming, biking, or running. My heart was beating outside of my chest as I took my first training run on the infamous Queen Kamehameha Highway. As I was running in the blazing heat that resembled a steam room, goosebumps ran up and down my body. I was on holy ground. It had seemed impossible for a little girl from urban Germany who had mediocre talent at best. I had fantasized hundreds of hours about making it to this race, reaching the legendary finish line of the Ironman Hawaii and hearing those words that touch the hearts of so many: "You are an Ironman." Or woman, I suppose, but now is not the time to philosophize on lingering gender oppression.

There was no sleep the night before the race. Alex received a phone call from another woman he had begun seeing just as we were getting ready to sleep, but I doubt it made a difference. My mind was on that highway. I was concerned about the swim start, with over a thousand athletes all going the same way in the water, resulting in "the world's biggest washing machine." I felt pretty solid about the bike, as rolling hills and heat were usually just fine by me. I was downright afraid of the marathon. And so, I rose at 3 a.m. to slowly make my way to the start. One last huge plate of spaghetti for breakfast to finish off my carb-loading, and I found myself on the beach with butterflies like fighter jets in my stomach and my heart in my throat. I thought about my Muschka, my home-team swim coach, my family, and friends. And there she was: Paula Newby-Fraser, casually warming up in the water. A day prior I had obtained her autograph during the Ironman Expo, and she had wished me good luck for race day. The hero from my bedroom walls was now in the water next to me.

The last minutes before the start seemed endless, and the cannon came as a relief. Almost panicked, I sprinted out of the crowd with just one thought in mind: "I can't get hurt. I have to finish this race. Who knows if I'll ever get to be back here again?". The swim flew by with a mixture of adrenaline and fear, and before I knew it, I was on the highway in the aero position just pedaling away.

Hawaii 2001, a humbling 112-mile bike ride.

Suddenly, there she was, like a fantasy from a boring training day, the Queen of Kona passing me on the bike. My heart jumped with excitement. I could not believe I was racing next to her. In a surge of disbelief and even more adrenaline, I began my pursuit, always a sufficient distance behind her to avoid disqualification for drafting. I stayed in that spot almost up to the halfway turning point, a remarkable accomplishment for a rookie. But it was also a horrible rookie mistake. I would soon be paying for it, and the currency was going to be pain, humility, and agony.

The inevitable outcome of my short-lived world class triathlete moment was a dreadful ride back to the second transition zone in Kona. The wind had turned and was now coming head-on like a blow dryer set on hot. My legs began to feel like spaghetti and shook a little here and there. The highway seemed twice as long on the way back. And I knew … I knew I had messed up and I was running out of gas even before the dreaded marathon. But I had to finish; this was still my dream. I parked my bike and limped into the transition tent, carefully putting on my running shoes while adding more sunscreen and downing what must have been my seventh and eighth liters of riptide-flavored purple Gatorade. Then, it was off the bench and out on the run course.

My legs felt like they were not mine and were barely obeying my brain telling them to run. It was like someone had stolen the bicycle right out from underneath me. I shuffled, tripped a little, jogged and finally reached mile marker one of 26. I could not help but laugh as I was tearing up. This all seemed like a cruel joke, and there was absolutely no possible way these legs would carry me over the next 25.2 miles. But I kept jogging down Alii Drive where the pros were zooming back out on the highway on the other side already. Alii Drive provided some much-needed shade, and between the orange slices and the ice cubes I placed in my running cap, there was a little bit of relief and hope. I made my way back on the highway and to the dreaded "Natural Energy Lab," a roughly 4-mile stretch of highway closed to spectators and the media, an intimate secret shared just among us athletes. Without going into graphic details, this is a place to attend to physical needs.

Shuffling along Alii Drive, about 8 miles down.

Here, it is OK to get sick, to cry, to walk. Upon exiting the Energy Lab, athletes pass the "makeup table,", a garden hose that provides cleansing relief and makes the racers presentable again. From here, it is just a few more miles back to town. The sun was setting, and my heart was sinking, because this meant I was way above the time I had hoped to achieve. I would not even break 12 hours. My world became disorganized, and as the dark settled in so did the confusion in my mind. As a German, I would always have to convert miles into kilometers to have a feel for how far I had left. Now and then, I would see mile markers or ask others "How much further?"

I would receive the answer, but by the time I would try to remember the conversion, I had forgotten the number. I was freezing cold on the dark highway that was still radiating heat. Then came the moment that made it all worth it: the turn into Kona and the crowds carrying me through the last mile. It was a moment I now wanted to last forever. My finisher photo did not show me smiling but crying tears of humility and disbelief and gratitude. Even though things went different from how I planned them, I was an Ironman, even if not a very fast one.

The year following the Ironman was anticlimactic. Another Ironman Hawaii qualification at the Ironman Lanzarote and another entirely unremarkable running death led me to decide I would never be able to run fast enough to really be a successful, moneymaking pro. My eating had been up and down for years — a steady passenger, hidden in the dark, too unthinkable to imagine for those who only saw the athlete. I wanted out. In August 2002, I left triathlon behind. Following a devastating break up from Alex, I was also hoping to find a boyfriend outside of the sport and some kind of normalcy in hopes of shaking the dark passenger once and for all.

For the first time in my life, at age 23, I was going to have a normal life. I attended a few parties and started Saturday night clubbing with friends. On one of those outings, at a local club close to the Heidelberg Olympic Training Center, I noticed a tall and handsome American soldier named Scott. He was quite drunk at the end of the night, and I happened to be our driver that evening, so I brought him back to his barracks safely. We exchanged numbers and ended up going on a few dates.

He was different from all the athletes in my life. He had played some basketball in college, but his life was not structured around training and nutrition schedules. While the Army certainly structured his life a lot, he was carefree otherwise. He was always up for doing something on the weekends, exhibiting a freedom I knew little about, and this freedom was intoxicating. Finally, there was someone who did not care about my race or training schedule. Someone I could just be with. And so, I fled my sport and entered a whirlwind of a new life. We fantasized about moving to America and getting married — the great escape. I traveled to one last Ironman Hawaii, and he deployed to Kuwait and then Iraq for several challenging months. When he came home, we ran away to Denmark and got married, 11 months after we met. We had barely spent 4 months together. Just like that, I was going to have a real life.

Chapter 3

Lessons from Being Lost on Land

The thing with dark passengers is that they are not easily lost, and mine followed me solidly across the Atlantic. Our newlywed life was hectic, as we had barely two months to prepare for a move across continents. We arrived in Colorado Springs with our suitcases and stayed in a local hotel while looking to buy a home. We quickly found a ranch starter home in a suburban neighborhood that consisted entirely of three types of houses that had been built in mere weeks. They were quite different from the old brick and mortar buildings of my hometown. As Scott returned to work, I spent my days in suburbia, and it did not take long until I realized I needed to do something. Anything.

I had heard the rumor that America was the land of opportunity and that anyone could work their way up — even without an education. I had always been an A and B student, even when I missed most of my last two years travelling for my sport. I had taken a few classes at the University of Mannheim and the University of Heidelberg but never stayed put at home long enough to really get involved in a degree-seeking program. And now at 24, I thought of myself as too old for an education. I took my stack of resumes to the local mall and quickly was hired as a jewelry sales assistant, a job I immediately found more painful than the Ironman Hawaii. I was particularly bad at talking people into buying overpriced jewelry that I personally viewed as entirely unnecessary. I befriended the security guards, whom I envied for at least being able to walk through the mall. And when an opening became available, I joined the security team. It turned out that walking the mall for 10 hours a day while explaining where the restroom was about 100 times a day was *also* not the fulfillment of the American dream my naïve mind had envisioned.

Discouraged, I sought help via a spousal re-employment program at Fort Carson, where Scott was stationed. I took some basic reading and math comprehension tests, and the Korean lady in charge yelled at me: "You smart! You college!" I tried to explain that I was too old and had no money, and that this was an impossibility. She insisted and handed me scholarship papers.

My husband was not opposed to the idea, and I enrolled in Pike's Peak Community College around the same time I found out I was expecting. Scott worked on weekdays and would spend his evenings and weekends in front of the television digesting the abundant American sports channels. While he was a devoted Patriots and Red Sox fan, he also enjoyed any other American football, baseball, or basketball games — professional and college — as well as the pre-and post-game shows. Long story short: There was always something highly relevant on the TV I slowly came to hate. I was lonely, and I was very far from home. Muschka cried when I called her to tell her I was expecting. They were not tears of joy; I think she knew I would not be able to just "come home." And since we spoke on the phone every day, she already knew I was lonely, and things were not what I had dreamt they would be.

You may wonder how the dark passenger, my eating disorder, was doing. It was thriving on the loneliness and isolation, and I no longer had my triathlon training as a coping mechanism. I still worked out an hour a day, either at Fort Carson's gyms or running through suburbia, but swimming was a rare occurrence. After all, I was an adult now, and I was not planning on ever swimming competitively or doing triathlons again. The "hunger games" took up a lot of my overflowing mental energy and worked as an effective numbing agent shielding me from reality. I also tried to spend as much time as possible at the community college, which I loved. I crammed the work of two years into one and was excited that I was receiving As in all my classes. It was not that I was a genius; rather, I had been prepared for academic success by the rigorous German Protestant private school that had tortured me with Latin, French, English and all the hard sciences. Muschka, who had lost everything in the war, always told me that knowledge is the one thing no one can take away from you.

My days consisted of working out, spending all day on campus, and returning to the house that did not really feel like home. All the while, the dark passenger tightened his grip on my mind, and I slowly was less and less able to eat at all. I had hoped that being pregnant would finally silence the dark passenger, as it was now so vital to eat well, and there was no pressure to be at a certain weight. But my mind rebelled at the idea of gaining weight, and with the lack of a social support system, I spent way too much time in this mind, which can be such a dangerous place. No amount of studying could quiet the thoughts, which are by far the most tormenting aspect of any eating disorder. They were omnipresent.

When should I eat? What should I eat? What shouldn't I eat? How many calories should I allow myself? How many calories had I eaten? Should I double count? Am I looking fat? Are these clothes too tight? I think my wrists are starting to look bigger!

It was a special kind of hell that only few can imagine. The true irony was that none of it had even the slightest thing to do with actual nutrition or actual appearance. My eating disorder functioned as an obsessive-compulsive disorder in the way my mind created rules and rituals that became a rapidly shrinking prison cell. Similarly, my rules and mind games became more elaborate the lonelier and more afraid I was. I believe it started with my intensely painful relationship with Alex and the lack of support outside the sport creating an emotionally painful climate, and my mind found a strategy to numb the pain and focus elsewhere. The cost was high – while the pain dissipated, so did all my real ties to the world. It all became a massive theater production in which I got up daily to pretend to be like all the others.

My son, Ashton, was born almost 10 weeks early and by the grace of God, healthy. But he was long and skinny, a stature he has kept to this day. (He's 15 now, and his 6'3'' frame weighs barely 125 lbs.) Some of the medical staff at Fort Carson were concerned. They noted my lack of weight gain, my two ER visits after passing out while shopping on post, and my spouse missing some of the pregnancy appointments he probably should have attended. They knew I was not well and referred me to a local counselor I started seeing weekly. Like several physicians I had reached out to over the years, the counselor told me I was looking great and to just eat healthy. They all had a profound misunderstanding of the nature of the territory in which I was trapped.

Following Ashton's birth, I completed my associate degree, but that was the last thing I would accomplish for a while. Aided by some post-partum depression, the dark passenger had grabbed the wheel and was now driving. I essentially stopped eating altogether and had great difficulty digesting fluids. I would regularly lose consciousness at home and crash to the floor. Scott was a much better father than he was a husband, and he was already dreaming of our baby boy becoming an NBA star while buying little basketball jerseys.

On yet another ER visit at Fort Carson, I crossed paths with an amazing young physician who had done a rotation in psychiatry. I will never forget that moment. I explained to him what was happening, and instead of just telling me to eat or that I was thin enough, he was highly alarmed. He located a treatment facility, the Eating Disorder Center of Denver, and was set on getting treatment at the facility approved by the insurance company. I still recall him yelling at the insurance representative on the phone: "If she was drinking, she would have been at the Betty Ford Center yesterday!" Part of me did not want to leave Ashton, but the physician convinced me that I would lose a lot more than 8 weeks with Ashton if I did not get well.

Jan. 5, 2005 is a date I will not forget. I panicked as we drove to the center, but I knew following my physician's advice was going to be vital in kicking the dark passenger out of the vehicle. My intake with the psychiatrist, a well-known eating disorder specialist, was simply remarkable. Eating disorders are notoriously difficult to treat because they become such an integral part of sufferers' emotional structure that getting them to buy into treatment is a major challenge. As I sat there in his office, I knew I wanted help, but I also knew I did not want to be forced to eat or gain weight, and the ambivalence was terrifying me.

The psychiatrist began by telling me what he already knew about me from my medical records. He was impressed by my involvement in sports and cleverly used my identity as an athlete to get my cooperation. "Well, if you had the willpower to compete in the Ironman," he said, "then you have the willpower to do this. Recovery is your race now, and I need you to make it your first five priorities." He spoke a language I understood.

My eight weeks in treatment are a blur now, but my days consisted of scheduled, therapist-supervised mealtimes as well as group and individual therapy sessions. Weekends brought visits from my husband and Ashton.

We slowly untangled my issues: depression and anxiety paired with grief over my distant relationship with my parents, and a father who was extremely critical. As my psychiatrist put it: "You brought your father with you to America." The overarching lesson here was that we cannot outrun our dark passengers; unaddressed, they will follow us to the end of the world. I was ready for change and had the help I needed. The colors came back into my life.

When I returned home in April 2005, I was different, and it rocked the boat. My intense dreams in recovery about swimming resulted in special permission to swim limited amounts in exchange for consuming nutritional shakes to make up for the burnt calories. I became a regular at the Fort Carson pool and the local 24-hour fitness center. I had lots of good bonding time with my baby boy. However, the relationship with my husband was cold and disengaged. He resented me for having left him hanging during my weeks in treatment, and I resented him as much as I had come to resent ESPN and all the other sports channels that were the focal point of his life.

The thing about recovery is that it has a ripple effect. You can keep things the same and relapse into your prior prison, or you can make the changes necessary to move forward. In my case, that meant realizing that my marriage had failed. Scott and I talked a lot and ultimately agreed to go our separate ways. I had no idea where to go or what to do next.

I enrolled at Colorado State University in Pueblo with the goal of getting my bachelor's in psychology, and with my prior credit hours transferring, it would take me about 2 years. One day after class, the neuroscience professor pulled me aside. I had missed an assignment, and I never, ever missed an assignment. In tears, I explained to her what was happening. I had no money and no job and a baby boy. My family was in Europe, but I could not go home because the court would not allow me to take my child out of the country permanently.

She arranged for me to move on campus, and I got a job in her rat laboratory injecting rats with different solutions. I remember driving my rented U-Haul truck to Pueblo, about 30 minutes south of Colorado Springs, with Ashton buckled in the passenger seat and tears flowing. I felt lost on a different planet, an alien. But over time, a new routine of co-parenting and child exchanges became normal, and with student loans and small jobs, I was getting by. I was once again swimming for an hour every day, and it helped. As I approached graduation, the same professor who hired me for

21

her lab encouraged me to apply for a Ph.D. program, so I applied for psychology doctorate programs across the United States.

I was accepted at Colorado State University in Fort Collins. My ex had moved to Denver, and Fort Collins was only about an hour away, so we would be able to make it work. Unable to afford two daycare bills, I became the weekend and vacation parent, which I liked because I got to focus on my work and had quality time with my boy. Little did I know that Fort Collins would be the place where new athletic dreams were to be born.

My parents visiting the Colorado State Campus.

Chapter 4

Lessons from Colorado Mountain Lakes

I moved into Colorado State's graduate student housing and found quite the international community – my immediate neighbors were from China, Russia and Oman, and some of them had brought their families. Everyone was invested in their studies and just as broke as me. Ashton made a young friend named Ali from Oman, and those two terrors on trikes made a game of hiding in random places. This prompted several large-scale search efforts by me and Ali's mother, who otherwise rarely left the apartment and wore a long burka when she did.

I loved graduate school. I loved the diversity and the community and my coursework. I found the professors inspiring and was fortunate to have an Italian professor, an exceptionally hard-working woman and single parent, accept me as part of her research team and mentor my master's thesis. A fierce feminist, she was fluent in Italian, Hebrew, and English and constantly questioned socio-cultural norms in general and gender norms in particular. My thesis examined the American phenomenon of high suicide-by-firearm rates among older Caucasian men. My mentor suggested the root cause for this phenomenon had to do with American gender socialization: Socio-cultural scripts dictate that men must be independent and that it is shameful to ask for help. I am not certain I can call myself a feminist, as for me (for some entirely irrational reason) it has a flavor of disliking men, and if anything, I adore men. I do find it telling we choose our young men to die for us and that men are often heavily burdened with the pressure to provide. Gender discrimination most certainly works both ways, and I always really preferred to be a free spirit — whatever that may mean.

One day, I heard about an annual 10K swim that was happening at the Horsetooth Reservoir, a mountain lake just a few miles west of the Fort Collins campus. My longest practice had been somewhere around 8K, years ago, and certainly not in one piece. I loved the challenge and signed up.

Training made studying possible. My school days usually consisted of about 10 hours of reading and writing, allowing me to keep my weekends free for Ashton. The only way I was able to tolerate sitting still and concentrating was to start my day in a mild state of physical exhaustion, a method that works for me to this day.

In the process of signing up for the event, I met its diligent hosts, Joe Bakel and Professor George Thornton. They had personal communication with each and every swimmer, and Joe advised me to get some cold-water exposure, as the lake would typically not get much warmer than the upper 60s to low 70s. At the pre-swim pasta party, I met a Colorado man that had swum the English Channel, and I learned that this was Joe's dream as well. Naturally, my adventurous mind and its busy wheels started to spin.

Every dream begins with a fantasy that one is not too afraid to believe in, no matter how crazy the world might think we are. My problem has always been a complete openness to what many would consider crazy ideas. I never took no for an answer, and somewhere between my emotional intensity and my mind lacking the limits of normalcy, these adventures become possible. However, this mindset is as dangerous as it is inspiring and has served me very poorly in some romantic relationships in which the parameters are so different from sports. There are areas in life where a fantasy-prone mind that believes it can conquer anything is taught painful lessons about what it can and cannot control.

The 10K swim was cold, but I think I was too nervous and elated to notice. It had been 6 years since I had last participated in any kind of race, and I felt like I had returned home. I finished somewhere towards the front of the middle of the pack but never had a chance of winning. Meanwhile, I worked up the nerve to talk to Joe about his English Channel training. He told me a small group of swimmers met at 4 in the morning and without a wetsuit at another local mountain lake to train about 9 months out of the year. I soon found myself on the banks of said mountain lake in cool and dark morning air, seriously doubting my sanity yet again.

Horsetooth 10k euphoria. I am back.

A note about my relationship to temperature: Muschka, having survived several extremely harsh and cold war winters with minimal heating, was determined to never be cold again, and she kept not only my little heart but also my body warm. It was always tropical in her apartment, and I must have had the world's heaviest down blanket. (I have been trying to find a similar one in the United States for years, and even though I am in the land of limitless stuff, I have not found anything like it.) Cold was my declared nemesis, and it had plagued me at triathlon races in Hamburg and in Geradmere, France, where the Alpine cold made me shake so hard on the bike I could not steer it safely on the descents and was unable to finish the race.

Joe was typically accompanied by another swimmer, a family physician. I found relief in that, as I strongly felt a medical emergency might be impending at any moment. As I walked into the water, my heart was pounding and my skin, burning. I stood hip-deep in the water waiting for my legs to go numb until I realized I had better get going to avoid being left behind in the dark. When I jumped all the way into the water, the cold shocked my body and knocked the breath right out of me. My head popped out of the water with a good measure of panic, and I wondered if this was what a heart attack felt like. I kept sprinting, and my skin began to burn, a not entirely unpleasant sensation. Somehow, I settled into a stroke, and as I slowly realized I was not dying (yet), it actually felt invigorating. Gliding quietly through a moonlit mountain lake left me feeling fierce and tickled my love for adventure.

I became a 4 a.m. regular at the mountain lake and secretly began toying with thoughts of swimming the English Channel. There were a few additional perks to open water swimming. Being chubby was a sign of the ability to withstand cold, and while I was not chubby by any means, I did not have to worry about the dark passenger getting any ideas of returning. Also, exact distance is difficult to measure in open water, and every swim comes with unique weather conditions and currents. That eliminated the frantic hunt for seconds, so common in pool events, so nothing was going to distract me from the enjoyment of just swimming. And the open water taught my compulsive mind that while we can prepare to an extent, there is always a humbling and uncontrollable element to our swims. We are all just tolerated guests in the water — and even on this planet — fragile beings, miraculously alive in a hostile world full of threats to our small bodies.

But the cold was only one challenge involved in swimming the English Channel. Although the straight-line distance from Dover, England, to Calais, France is 21 miles, currents pushing swimmers laterally can make the distance typically traveled as much as 36 miles. I began looking for a steppingstone challenge and signed up for a 13-mile swim around the island of Key West, Florida. I had not really travelled anywhere besides my home in Germany since my Ironman days and, as I flew from Denver to Miami, I felt more alive than I had in a good while. I had bought a travel guide for Key West that lovingly described it as an "alternative lifestyle island". As I boarded the small plane from Miami to the Keys, I noticed the passengers included many same-sex couples and several amazing drag queens who traveled in full show attire. I was thrilled to discover there was a safe haven for diversity in gender and sexual orientation in the most southern place of the United States, and I was so delighted to spend an entire week in this special place. Key West now owns my heart, and it was love at first sight.

The water glistened in every shade of my favorite color, teal, and its warmth and saltiness provided a buoyant feeling that made swimming feel even more weightless. The circumnavigation was a dream of a swim, not only because of the beautiful waters, but also the beauty of the tiny island and its people. Little art galleries, unique restaurants, and a feeling that people could truly be themselves made this place feel magical to me.

Following Key West, I was encouraged that I could swim at least 6 hours. I began to do serious research about the English Channel and learned about the "Triple Crown of Open Water Swimming", which consists of the "Swim Around Manhattan Island", the Catalina Channel and the English Channel. I would tackle them in that order, the order of increasing difficulty. And so, the Colorado mountain lakes became my temporary home and a centerpiece for my life, which otherwise consisted of my studies and being a single parent of a little boy who made it all worthwhile with his blond curls, big brown eyes and gentle temperament.

Chapter 5

Lessons from the Hudson River

Joe's wife, a tremendously talented marathon runner, kindly let me borrow her husband to be on my crew for the Swim Around Manhattan Island. Joe has sacrificed his time and payed out of pocket many times over the years to be a reliable and invaluable crew member. As an engineer, he brings calm and rationality to the boat, while I tend to be a little more impulsive and intense, so he adds a much-needed perspective to the crew.

In early summer 2010, Joe and I travelled from Denver to New York City. Given my grad student budget, the accommodations could be charitably described as "oddly invigorating": We ended up in a youth hostel across from Central Park sleeping with our valuables in our pillowcases.

New York City's hustle and bustle amplified my already busy and fast-paced mind, creating a mildly manic state. I was eager to meet my boat captain, an attractive NYFD firefighter, in person, as I had communicated solely online with him. Walking across Times Square, I was reminded of a human ant farm, and the fact it was enclosed by water seemed to make it the perfect place for cowards to attack. The city smelled of the river and of concrete, and as we rode a largely empty subway on race day to the start of the swim at Battery Park, my mind was spinning.

As an introvert, I need a certain amount of solitude, quiet and familiarity to get my mind to the right place. Here, in the "city that never sleeps", I felt exposed and overwhelmed. I felt like I could not retreat or control the pace around me, and this feeling of exposure left me dizzy and disoriented.

The start of a race is often a relief after dealing with the agony of nervous buildup to it and jumping into a cold and gray Hudson River was no different. I thought of Mannheim, my hometown, and our modest little training pool. And here I was: Kathi was casually swimming by the Statue of Liberty. I could not help but laugh at how incredibly unlikely and amazing it all felt to me.

As we set off into the river, I was accompanied by my captain and two kayakers to my left and right, who shielded me from the heavy boating traffic on the Hudson River. Most marathon swims are devoid of sensory input, but this one is certainly the exception. The "Swim Around Manhattan Island" is about 28 kilometers, but the heavy current assist reduced my time in the water to 8 hours and some change, and I was astounded at how that current made me feel like I was zooming around the island. Talk about feeling fast.

My focus typically turns inwards during long swims, but this one was entirely different. There was much to see and absorb: Yankee Stadium, Columbia University, Ground Zero and the George Washington Bridge – where I had to stop for a bit while NYPD talked a jumper off the bridge. It was an unreal whirlwind, and even the memory of the swim still feels dizzy and manic.

Past the George Washington bridge and heading back to Battery Park.

Elated after the swim, my NYFD boat captain and I closed the after-swim party bar down and set out into the NYC nightlife, hitting some Irish pubs, and finally having breakfast at a Stanton Island diner. I did not want the good conversation to end, but by sunrise, reality had returned, and Joe was relieved I had not gotten lost in the Big Apple during my slightly manic episode. We hit the Guggenheim Museum, another mind-blowing, intellectually stimulating experience, and then returned to Colorado.

New York was an incredible rush and confirmed that I live for adventure and challenge. I passionately believe the moment we become stagnant is when our spirit starts to decay. The true beauty of personal challenges is that they are driven from within. I have never been an Olympian, and swimming has never paid my bills. I simply want what challenges me as a human because it makes me feel alive. I agree with ultra-marathon runner Dean Karnazes, who has remarked that people today are "too convenienced"; that is, it is not our natural state to not have to struggle. Life is inherently difficult, painful and a fight for survival. Our fragile bodies have adapted for survival, while our mind has become the weak link. Humanity today feels it is our birthright to be happy, to own everything and to not have to experience pain, struggle, or loss. And our filtered social media world reinforces that view when it only shares the flattering angles of life.

My point here is that I am an addict, and though I have chosen a less harmful poison than some, my pursuit for adventure is as imperfect as is my performance. Every single elated high has a corresponding low. One moment, I am a triumphant channel swimmer, and the next, I am an equally devastated divorcee and lost soul.

Chapter 6

Lessons from the Catalina Channel

My decision to go into the mental health field was driven by my own history and exposure to therapy, which for me personally was a powerful transformative process. While I tremendously enjoyed graduate school, the fact that a graduate research or teaching assistant makes little money while I was accumulating a significant amount of student loans was a burden. Americans seem to have a much greater comfort with the concept of debt, but German culture is typically much more conservative when it comes to loans and credit cards. On the heels of my master's degree, another 2-3 years to earn my doctoral degree would have easily doubled my student loans while making a small impact on my earning potential. The thought of leaving early to find a regular paying job was now on my mind.

As part of my vocational psychology course, I was to shadow someone in their chosen profession and prepare a case-study paper. A Brazilian friend of mine named Kenny, who had kayaked for me at the Horsetooth 10K, was a local police officer and invited me to do a ride-along. It became quickly apparent that his job was diverse and challenging, and he encouraged me to apply to several police departments across Colorado. My feminist professor was elated at the idea that I could enter a male-dominated career with some unique insights that I owed to my graduate program. And to me, it sounded like an adventure, and I was never one to turn down a challenge.

While I finished my master's thesis and waited on job offers, I found a creative, cost-effective way to swim California's Catalina Channel: as a trio with two male swimmers who swam at roughly my pace. We would split the escort boat cost three ways and make our way from Catalina Island to the shores of Los Angeles swimming side-by-side. It took us some convincing to receive permission for this idea, but we were soon swimming side by side through Colorado mountain lakes trying to synchronize our strokes for the long journey ahead.

A few short months later, I found myself on a smoggy, six-lane Los Angeles highway driving at a walking pace to the pier where we would start our swim. None of us had had time for much sightseeing so most of my Catalina memories revolve around our swim. It is a nighttime endeavor due to heavy daytime boating traffic and currents, and it was my first-time swimming in the dark anywhere besides Colorado mountain lakes.

A large dive boat with the ironic name "Bottomscratcher" took us out to the island. I tried to sleep a little in my bunk under deck, but my heart was racing and my head spinning as usual before an adventure. That was ok, as anxiety helps me get myself into the heightened arousal state that helps me to mobilize all my physical resources. This swim would be the longest swim I had done thus far, a full 21 miles, and the water temperature was only a few degrees above the English Channel. Many told me that if I could swim Catalina, I would be able to swim the English Channel, provided the notoriously fickle English weather would allow it.

Cliff, myself, and Jeff (left to right) plus Catalina crew.

Shortly after midnight, we stood on the dark deck overlooking a dark ocean. To honor the occasion, I had purchased a new swimsuit that was a very snug fit and would have been much better suited for a 100-meter freestyle race rather than a channel swim. It was a rookie mistake that would leave me with sea lice bite marks where my suit had been for weeks after the swim. You see, sea lice tend to cling to fabric, particularly tight fabric, so I ended up providing a fantastic cruise vacation for multiple large families of the aquatic parasites.

As I stood there in the dark, my two fellow swimmers, Cliff and Jeff, reminded each other to be careful about the kelp. Just as I was ready to ask what kelp was, they jumped overboard, and I followed. We had to swim a short distance to the beach on Catalina Island, and all the while my mind was stuck on what "kelp" was and why I needed to worry about it. In German, the word "Kalb" means "calf," so I was solidly prepared to swim into some sort of a large sea cow.

As we got closer to the beach Jeff began to curse about the kelp, and seconds later I found myself in heaps and heaps of – well, some type of sea grass that was apparently called kelp. Massive relief.

Standing on Catalina Island, I could see the lighthouse about 21 miles away. It seemed so close that it was hard to imagine we would be swimming through the entire night to reach it. Shortly after midnight, our small formation set of into the cold Pacific — Cliff on my right and Jeff on my left. The dive boat searchlight shining on us illuminated the dark ocean, and I saw numerous square jellyfish underneath us. Connected in lines, they looked like some bizarre cell sample under a microscope. I could also hear the clicking noises of dolphins underneath us, but the dark made it impossible to spot them. Meanwhile, I was about to learn why we had difficulty obtaining permission for a trio crossing.

All three of us took breaks from swimming for food and drink. We received these "snacks" from a kayak that was, in turn receiving them from the main boat every 30 minutes. The water was quite choppy, and in the dark, it was difficult for the kayaker to hand each of us our preferred nutrition. What would probably be a 30-second stop for an individual swimmer was more of a 2-minute endeavor for our trio, and on one occasion, the kayak capsized, sending us scrambling to safe our food from the ocean.

Now while a long break might seem quiet cozy, it also meant treading water until we were good to go again. During this time, blood flowing out of each swimmer's core and into their legs, combined with the lack of motion, contributed significantly to a loss in body heat. This loss of body heat meant our bodies were on borrowed time.

With the long breaks, I struggled tremendously with the cold. Jeff and Cliff, both heavier built, seemed to not have this problem, but I could think of little else. I scanned the horizon frantically, but all was black. Finally, many hours later, I was able to see a slight line of light separating the black ocean from the black sky. The light brought hope of a new day and warmth. With the sunrise lifting my spirit, things seemed less grim as we swam into the morning. But instead of sun warming my back, fog with no trace of sunshine made it difficult to see. Cliff was elated and had to slow himself down to stay in formation, and while Jeff did seem tired, he did not seem cold. But I was struggling.

I thought about not wanting to let Jeff or Cliff down and about not wanting to tell those who warned us against the swim that they were right. I thought of my little boy, of how I was taking time and money away from him to be here, about how technically I could not afford these things and about needing to finish what I started. And then, as the cold worsened, the best I could do was count to 10. Over and over and over. Finally, the words I had longed to hear came: We were only a few miles from shore. The brief euphoria was quickly halted when we reached the continental shelf, an area where upwelling brings cold water from the bottom to the surface of the ocean. It made for a cold welcome to the shore, but I was too close to quit. I kept counting, often not making it to 10 before losing track as hypothermia-related confusion began to sink in.

Finally, the Bottomscratcher anchored as we swam to shore accompanied by our kayak. On the pebble beach, Cliff's five children and his wife waved frantically, making me smile. Our exit from the water was less than elegant, as we tried to stand on the slick, uncomfortable pebbles while the surf knocked us off balance. Jeff began to make headway on all fours and, stealing his moment of illumination, so did I. Then the horn came from the boat signifying the finish as Cliff's family cheered. We were finally on land after 10 hours and 41 minutes. I immediately sat and curled up, as the wind was now biting, and I wanted nothing more than a warm shower. But first, we would be making our way back into the water to swim back out to the Bottomscratcher. Fury rose inside me at the idea of having to swim another 300 meters back. I was done.

Jeff and I, on slippery rocks and fighting for balance.

I do nott remember much about getting back on board, but I was helped into a tiny shower, and someone else helped me wrap myself in blankets and laid me down on deck, just above the engine. It was a nice, warm spot in which I immediately fell asleep. I woke up to excited yelling and saw that we had a dolphin escort as our boat traveled back to the pier. I looked at Jeff, who had been stung in the face by a jellyfish and looked a little rough, and we exchanged the biggest grin. We had done it. I'll be damned.

Shortly after my Catalina adventure, I left graduate school and returned to Colorado Springs, where I excitedly waited to begin the police academy. I shared a small apartment with a roommate to save money for the English Channel. I reserved a 2012 spot with famous pilot Mike Oram, an English fisherman, who has brought more swimmers across the English Channel than any other pilot. I had two years to save and train.

One day while training, I met some athletes looking for a woman to join their team for a 24-hour adventure race in Moab, Utah. I was a bit worried about the land navigation component and the mountain biking, but being addicted to adventure, I agreed.

A few days before the race, on an online blind date, I met Destin, a career soldier, and Green Beret from Louisiana. We talked about my weekend plans: an adventure race in Utah to benefit a wounded soldier in recovery.

He was fascinated and asked to come with. I was a little worried about committing to a 10-hour, one-way drive with a stranger, but we had a ball on the way to Moab. We shared adventure stories, and 10 hours later, I knew a lot more about ranger school, special forces selection and Louisiana food. We met the rest of the team in Moab: another Green Beret (a major), an Army social worker and the wounded veteran who inspired our adventure.

The race consisted of a short river swim, followed by several hours in kayaks, on foot and, finally, mountain biking. And personality clashes. The major seemed a bit nervous about the swim, and we had to wait for him on shore while boarding the kayaks. I shared the kayak with the social worker, and we got along quite well, both complaining only about how cold our hands were while kayaking. In the boat behind us, struggling to keep up was the disgruntled major, who at some point swung his paddle at the vet and asked that I share the boat with him. He mumbled something about weight distribution, but the math did not add up, and I stayed where I was. The major did handle the land navigation exceptionally well, even though I was quite annoyed by his downright refusal to jog, insisting on walking instead.

As the sun set, we got on our mountain bikes. I had fallen into water earlier, and as the dark settled into the wild, lonely Utah canyon, I was once again cold. For some time, I rode next to the major, who kept suggesting that a better use of my evening would be having a nice dinner with Destin or sleeping in a warm bed. After a few hours of this and about 18 hours into the race, struggling to climb endless mountains with a bike that seemed heavier by the hour, I finally stopped and announced I was done. In retrospect, I think the major himself wanted to spend the night in a warm bed but needed to save face. My announcement was met with fury by the wounded soldier, who screamed at me "The infantry does not quit!". I quietly got back on my bike, where I spent the next 8 hours paddling to a 26-hour finish, a respectable third place for our team.

Back in Colorado Springs, I dedicated the next spring to the police academy, which was a new challenge of an entirely different kind. I learned the classroom suited me more than the shooting range, as I had never fired a gun in my life and was truly struggling to make the minimum qualifications. I liked the comradery, which reminded me of sports. I admired the steadfastness and sacrifice of the experienced officers who ensured we all understood the huge responsibility we would be carrying when earning our badges. It was often humbling, and those lessons from the slow lane came in handy as I was humbled daily.

I learned what it felt like to be squirted with pepper spray and what it felt like to be on the receiving end of a taser, which I did not take gracefully. More pain came during our "Red Man" scenario, which mimics a call for service that escalates into a physical fight, challenging you to use what you learned in defensive tactics.

The entire scenario is a blur to this day, but I recall getting hit harder than I had ever been hit before. I remember panic and people screaming at me. I had managed to put the SWAT officer, who was wearing protective gear that prevented him from being able to tuck his chin, into a rear naked choke. When he attempted to tap out, I did not see it or hear the commands yelled at me. I accidentally choked him out, and my classmates were elated. Only one training officer, our range instructor, saw the problem with this – panic was dangerous, and I had not only panicked but also lost control.

Nevertheless, graduation day was a day of celebration attended by Destin, whom I had been seeing ever since Moab and who really encouraged me throughout the academy. But what I did not realize quiet yet was how different from the academy the reality of the profession would be. This adventure had no off-switch. I could not just climb in the boat or quit when I had enough. Those who stand between us and civil chaos or defend us in times of war do not have that luxury, and while I deeply wish we did not need them, the reality is that we do, and I am grateful for their sacrifice.

Chapter 7

Lessons from the English Channel

After graduating the police academy, I entered the world of being a patrol officer. I had navigated different countries and cultures, but this was a true culture shock. I knew I wanted to work where the need was greatest and ended up working the rougher part of town. My first big reality check happened while I was still in training with a senior officer. It would be the last time I would work in daylight for a few years.

While practicing traffic stops, I stopped a pickup truck with an expired plate driven by a white gentleman with a baby girl in the passenger seat. I asked him for his papers; he told me he was bringing the baby to daycare and had left his wallet at home. No big deal. I returned to the patrol car where my training officer told me to go back to the truck and get his Social Security number to verify his identity. A few seconds later, I was back telling my training officer the driver could not remember the entire number. In Germany, we have no such thing as Social Security numbers, and at the time, I did not realize every adult in the United States memorizes their social security number. We decided we would have to ask the gentleman to step out of the vehicle. As I walked back to the car, faster than I could comprehend, my training officer bolted by me, ripped the truck door open and pulled the gentleman out and flat onto the pavement. After a brief struggle, he was cuffed, searched, and detained in the back of our patrol car.

What I had not seen was the driver tilting towards the door pocket, in which there was a .45 caliber Judge Taurus revolver. Upon searching the vehicle, we found large amounts of methamphetamines as well as uncapped and used syringes within the reach of the toddler. In the interview room at the station, the gentleman admitted to dealing methamphetamines between New Mexico and Colorado and using his daughter as a "cover" to look less suspicious. He admitted that he had considered shooting me when I was walking back to the truck. Reality was getting real.

I learned the culture of the hood and what it means to live in poverty in one of the richest countries in the world. I learned that racial tensions are a long way from being resolved. I learned that in many poor African American families in the United States, there is a heartbreaking absence of men as role models, and if you need to really get a point across, you talk to the family matriarch, usually the mother or grandmother. I learned about the discrimination that Hispanic immigrants were facing, many of which working in construction, expected to build a suburban neighborhood in a matter of weeks in exhausting 15-hour days — yet being paid ridiculously little. I learned about addiction, prostitution, and mental illness. This was a far different universe from the ivory tower of graduate school.

While working nights in what we lovingly called "the Creek," I trained for the English Channel. It was less than optimal, with insufficient sleep and rare open water access, mostly in the small pool of a 24-hour gym. Destin and I had gotten married at the local courthouse during my time in the academy. With him being a solider and me being a cop, being married would ensure we had access to each other in an emergency, and in a worst-case scenario, he would be able to assist Ashton in accessing my life insurance money.

We got along well. He deployed often and was rarely home, and if he was home, we barely saw each other with him working days and me working from 5 p.m. until 3 a.m.. Despite work demands, I nevertheless trained consistently and intensely, but probably was putting in a lot less mileage than most.

In July 2012, Destin, Joe Bakel, and I arrived in Dover, England. For days I had been checking the weather forecast compulsively, as if it would magically change every 30 minutes. On the day of our arrival, the sky was blue and the water glassy — perfect conditions. However, a storm system was headed towards England and often, these storm systems do not move out for a few weeks. My swim window was closing while my anxiety was shooting sky-high. Mike Oram had signed up four swimmers for a 10-day "tide window." and I was Number 2 on the tide. This meant if there was a swimmable day, Number 1 would have the option to swim or wait and let someone else go.

We had been in Dover 24 hours, and I had slept one night (though we were all still very jet-lagged) when I received the call – Number 1, another American, had arrived the same day as me, and he needed to get over his jet lag and wanted to wait. Joe cautioned me that I had not slept enough, but there was no way I was going to say no. The remainder of the day was a whirlwind of buying groceries, packing supplies, and trying to rest. I managed to sleep a few hours before we walked down to the Dover Marina at 2 a.m., on July 25, 2012, all of us carrying totes of supplies. My pilot, Mike Oram, was supposed to arrive in his small fishing boat at 3 a.m. The air was cold and dark and reminded me of German fall days when the cold first starts to bite. I was bundled up heavily to preserve as much heat for as long as possible. This was going to be the coldest day of my life, yet I would encounter much colder in the years to come.

3 a.m. came and went, and no Mike Oram. Mind you, this swim had been booked for more than 2 years prior. I had saved for years and had travelled here all the way from Colorado, but no Mike Oram. No answer on his cell or home phone. I was ready to start crying. Joe did his best to keep me calm, and Destin made some jokes to lighten the mood, which did not go over well. I was fuming. Then, at about 4:30 a.m., the Gallivant pulled into the Marina, and Mike Oram arrived, as unshowered as he was unapologetic. He had slept and lived on the boat for a while getting as many swimmers across as the Channel Gods would allow. Luckily, he had an exceptionally nice looking, middle-aged, French skipper with a pearly white smile as his assistant, and that lightened my mood a little.

I got greased up with a lanolin-vaseline mix thought to aid in preserving body heat. It is most likely a stronger placebo than an actual heat retainer, but it was a nice barrier against the harsh water. About 5 a.m., I climbed off the boat and hit cold and dark water that shocked me wide awake. I climbed out of the water and onto the beach, as swim rules dictate swimmers' ankles must be out of the water at the start and finish. Mike tooted the horn, and off I went into the dark. No kayakers were needed; all support would be handled off the main boat. Our food delivery system was a broomstick with a plastic basket that Destin would hold out onto the water. It all seemed unreal as I swam next to the boat looking at Joe, Destin, and the French

41

skipper, all heavily bundled up in the morning cold while I was exposed to the elements. At least it was my element.

The dark was depressing and irritating, and I could not wait for daylight. I must have complained of being cold at every feed stop for the first few hours, until Joe finally told me there was nothing they could do for me, and I would either have to keep swimming or get out. So, I no longer shared my complaints and choice words with the crew. I will never forget the sunrise on the English Channel, which was a godsend. The sky was clear and with the rising sun, there was small comfort in light and just a little bit of warmth on my back. However, as we were in a busy shipping lane, we frequently passed large freight ships roughly 200 meters away. The freight ships would cause the water temperature to drop from an already unpleasant 60 degrees to the high 40s for a few, particularly miserable minutes.

About 6 hours in, I started cramping in my hip flexors, a deep-seated pain that caused my entire body to feel stiff. I tried stretching, I curled up into a ball, I did open flip turns, I drank more … nothing seemed to help, and I was losing speed and hope rapidly. Mike finally came on deck to see what was happening and unbeknownst to me, him and Joe decided to give me some Maxim, a maltodextrin powder, from a stash that Mike kept on board the Gallivant. Maltodextrin is a tasteless and short-chained carbohydrate that many swear by, but I preferred tasty little gels, popular among triathletes, and protein shakes. However, I was taking in too many calories and not enough water, underestimating the amount of water one loses in the cold by just exhaling. The Maxim did the trick: I recovered and settled into my rhythm again.

The water was green and murky with golden specks, and it seemed to be rushing underneath me, so much so I thought I was going backwards several times. My crew assured me we were making good progress. I wondered if they were lying to me. You see, Joe and I had agreed that while I would wear a simple stop watch to keep track of how long I had been swimming, the crew would not provide me with any information regarding distance to avoid the psychological devastation of losing ground due to tides or currents.

Around the 10- hour mark and in French waters, I started feeling pretty good. The sun was solidly on my back and had even warmed up the top layers of the water, causing me to stretch out my stroke longer to enjoy the surface water just a little bit more. Then finally, in the distance, I could see land for the first time. Swimmers try not to look at the beach they are

42

swimming towards, as the beach often looks deceivingly close, and it can be crushing to realize how long it will actually take to get there.

The trickiest part of the English Channel, where most swims are abandoned, is the last 2 miles before the coast, as one has to overcome a significant riptide to make it to shore. Mike Oram's specialty is timing the arrival just right and using his boat strategically to shield the swimmer from the current. Finally, I received the command "sprint now" and began to pick up the pace. My arms felt like they were receiving electric shocks, and it was challenging to break the movement pattern I had settled into for hours. We now took food breaks every 20 minutes. I got another "go faster" command, then another, and finally Mike was loudly hollering "Move your arse!" and several other fairly blunt things that had me a little surprised and a little ticked. But they had me moving.

I dug deep. I thought of my sprint days and of the pool and how it was all coming down to this moment. I thought of time spent training and money saved to be here. I thought of Ashton and Muschka, and how I would have to call her later to tell her I made it. Suddenly, we were right in front of the beach, and I saw Destin changing into swim trunks to swim the last 200 meters in with me, swimming an inelegant Army sidestroke.

It is rare to land on a sand beach when crossing the English Channel; some only get to touch rocks before returning to their boats. Not only did we hit a sandy beach, it was also a beach full of people enjoying this summer day. As I staggered out of the water, still covered in thick white chunks of the lanolin-vaseline mix and with a swollen face and purple hands and feet, a small crowd gathered around and began to stare at me like I was some bizarre alien. Finally, a man with a thick French accent asked me: "Did you swim here from England?" Beaming, I replied: "I sure did," and the small crowd erupted in excited clapping.

It was time to swim back to the boat, and as I re-entered the water, my elation and bliss were interrupted by a terrifying thought. How would I ever be able to top this? A wave of fear washed over me. What was I supposed to do now? Live a stagnant and boring life? The fear did not last long, as I was soon wrapped in a snug, warm and grease-stained sleeping bag. I really wanted to see the channel on the way back from the boat but quickly fell asleep.

Writing name and swim time on the White Horse wall is tradition.

Back in Colorado Springs, my police station was full of excitement, and I received congratulation emails from the chief of police, the deputy chiefs, and my commander. I even gave a small interview in uniform outside our station. Finally, a police story that was light-hearted and positive, a luxury we were afforded not nearly often enough. I quickly settled back into my daily routine but also decided I needed to immediately find a new goal to protect myself from being without direction. Originally, I had considered retiring from swimming after the English Channel but 2013 had everything but retirement in store.

Chapter 8

Lessons from the Pacific

Frantic to not become stagnant after the English Channel, I made 2013 an exceptionally event-heavy year. I started the year with an Ironman distance race triathlon on the beautiful island of Key West. The race was a grassroots event in its first year and not sanctioned by the World Triathlon Cooperation, so it did not hold the official title "Ironman." Of course, the legendary Ironman Hawaii started as a grassroots event — a few guys and gals on the beach trying to see if they had what it took to rise to the challenge. This spirit has always motivated me, but the mass marketing of the Ironman brand and the selling of the sport was off-putting. I am glad that marathon swimming remains a sideline sport that still has the grassroots flavor of simply embarking on a great adventure.

It was heaven to be in Key West, as it always is. Between the warm ocean and the warm people on Duval Street, the nightly sunset celebration on Mallory Square featuring acrobats and artists, and the excellent and uniquely Cuban influence cuisine, there is nothing left to wish for. As I write this, I am still trying to find ways to make this place my home.

The race itself was humbling to say the least, likely the result of some English Channel inspired delusions of grandeur. I had run a bit but barely had time to bike. Thinking I was a natural on the bike anyway, I figured my swim endurance would probably transfer. It did not. 12 years prior, I spent about 20 hours a week cycling alone, and it turned out that spending about

2 hours a week on the bike was no match for an Ironman distance. I finished about 2 hours slower than in the good old triathlon days, and though I felt quite old and humbled, I quickly found relief in some tropical beverages and the colorful nightlife of Duval Street.

I also signed up for an open-water swimming stage race called SCAR in Arizona that April. The acronym stands for the four bodies of water to be conquered in four consecutive days: Saguaro Lake, Canyon Lake, Apache Lake, and Roosevelt Lake. SCAR is special in that, while marathon swimmers do not tend to travel in packs, here we did. I enjoyed the sense of community tremendously, except for sharing my sleeping quarters with fellow Coloradoan Sarah Thomas, who later became known for beating breast cancer and completing a world-record, out-of-this-world, four-way English Channel crossing in 2019. A terrific and humble person, Sarah is really fun to hang out with, but this woman knows no cold. From ceiling fans to air conditioning, I spent my nights shivering and trying not to whine and complain too much. The swims themselves were all surprisingly cold, given the Arizona heat, but most of the water is quite deep and moving, so in comparison to the hot air, it felt even more unpleasantly cold. I have two main SCAR memories: swimming by cacti and trying to secretly raise the thermostat temperature while Sarah, who throughout the event complained of being uncomfortably warm, was sleeping.

SCAR 2013, a rare bonding opportunity for marathon swimmers.

Another attempt at avoiding stagnation despite not being able to "top the Channel" was something I had never done before: a 50-mile trail run up and down the Colorado mountains, entirely above 10,000 feet, known as the Leadville 50-Miler. It was another very questionable idea.

The trails were technically challenging, and I lost track of how many times I rolled my ankles. Using the small portable bathroom on top of the mountain after 26 miles and barely being able to get back up, it was becoming clear this would be a long day. On the way down to the finish, a mountain storm brought lightning and hail and added to my misery. Finally, I tripped and fell on a small, winding path. Hands skinned and ribs bruised, I fought my way to the finish in just under 14 hours. Never again.

I obviously needed to stick with swimming. And I was tired of being cold. Researching my options, it seemed the Kaiwi Channel between Molokai and Oahu, Hawaii, would be ideal. At 26 miles and with water temps in the 80s, this would finally be another successful experience after a scatterbrained, directionless year.

That October, Destin and I were to stay on Oahu, and I was simply in heaven just being back in Hawaii. Training swims in the hotel bay were magical, and I enjoyed swimming with the sea turtles the Hawaiians lovingly call "honus" (for "long life"). I felt particularly good about this swim: I knew I could swim long, and without my nemesis, the cold, this should be fairly easy. I was neither too nervous nor too concerned as my 10-day swim window opened. But if I have learned one thing in all these years in endurance sports: It is that attitudes are for adjusting. And the Kaiwi Channel gods were going to be my merciless teachers.

Waiting for the green light on a swim as one's assigned swim time window passes is quiet aggravating. I must save money, vacation time, train accordingly, and usually have made tremendous sacrifices just to be at the swim location. My car is embarrassing to my son, I only buy necessary clothing, and we live very simply. So as the days passed, the mood grew increasingly tense.

After calling my crew guys every night for a week, on night eight I finally became upset: "When are they finally going to allow me to swim?", demanding an answer. I assumed that Kaiwi was like all the other channels, and that we would need the green light from the coastguard. My crew guy told me that while he recommended waiting at least another day, it was really just up to me. Panicking that my window was going to close without me ever even hitting the water, I announced we would swim the following day.

My boat captain had originally suggested I fly over to Molokai and spend the night there to meet him for a midnight start. I declined, telling him I would rather save a little money and take the 3-hour trip over to Molokai from Oahu with him on the boat. I also told him "I don't get seasick." Famous last words.

Sitting on Oahu pointing across the Kaiwi channel at Molokai.

As we set out into the channel the next evening at sunset, swells were about 4 to 6 feet, and the wind was steady. Our small fishing boat bounced up and down on the waves causing little drops that reminded me of that tickling pull in your stomach on a roller coaster. I had spent the whole day carbo-loading, eating ungodly amounts of spaghetti, and drinking a large green vegetable juice from a local juice shop. Without getting into too much graphic detail, I will just say think of the classic horror movie "The Exorcist." One more piece of advice: When you are desperately seasick and unable to refrain from abandoning your last meal, do so downwind, not upwind.

It was disastrous. My crew guys turned as green as the spaghetti around them. The smell was lingering and so was my nausea. I spent the majority of the ride to Molokai leaning over the side of the boat, apparently paying for every sin I had ever committed in my life. The crew and captain were concerned, but I had some hope that once in Molokai, I would be able to nap on the pier a bit and replenish some much-needed fluids. Wrong again.

Molokai is one of the few Hawaiian Islands that is not a typical tourist destination and, there is not a lot of infrastructure. There was no pier and no lights. While the boat was anchored, it was still moving in the chop, and sleep was not going to happen. Neither Destin nor my amazing crew — captain Matt Buckman and kayakers Jeff Kozovitch and Steve Haumschild – thought I was in any shape to swim. I thought of all the nights on patrol in the Creek and the eight grand it had cost me to be here and realized the fury in me was not going to let me leave without at least trying. I announced we were just going to start now.

I jumped off the boat into the murky ocean and made my way to the beach, only to realize we had some serious waves coming in. I did not want to be tumbled around in the dark to the point I would have difficulty finding my way to the surface. Steve followed me to the beach in his kayak. Standing on the completely dark beach, mad as hell, I began counting to learn the wave pattern. I was going to run in as the waves came in and then sprint — hopefully dodging the next big one and getting through the surf. Except that the run needed to be a shuffle to not step on any sea urchins or stingrays.

I counted, went for it, and made it. I paused to look for Steve when I saw his kayak, two green light sticks on each end, flipped around lengthwise by a large incoming wave. I tried to see the boat and realized it was several hundred meters away. While I could see them, I was not sure if they could see the tiny green blinking light attached to the back of my goggle straps. I felt utterly alone and a little panicked. I decided to stay where I was and holler for Steve, who eventually made it out as well.

And so shortly after midnight, we left a pitch-black Molokai behind to set out into a pitch-black ocean. I had swum at night before, but this was different. It was nearly a new moon, and the night was so dark that I felt like I was swimming in outer space. To make things even more surreal, my movements in the water caused golden light specks, which I later learned were caused by some type of plankton. Swimming blindly, I could not distinguish the water from the sky, nor could I sense when to breathe. I had given strict directions about wanting everything as dark as possible, with no light beams from the boat or the kayak, on the advice of a fellow swimmer.,

49

who years prior had been attacked by a cookie cutter shark. These cigar-shaped deep-sea creatures have a bite that resembles those little kitchen tools you use to cut melon balls. His theory in retrospect was that the beam his main boat had shone on him attracted first small, then medium-sized fish, until finally the entire food chain made an unlikely and unfortunate appearance resulting in him sustaining a rather severe bite to the calf area.

The nausea had miraculously evaporated the moment I jumped into the water, but I felt weak and shaky from hours of dry heaving. We stopped every 20 minutes, and between Pepsi, electrolyte supplements and lots of water, I started to feel OK and settled into a rhythm. The wind and waves were relentless, but word from the crew was that things should settle down by sunrise. So once again, I caught myself staring at the dark with the desperate desire to see that fine line of light that would slowly begin to separate the ocean from the sky. The sunrise boosted my morale, and I was just waiting for the ocean to calm down, for things to get easier, to be able to glide more and not struggle against the force of the waves with every stroke. No such luck. Noon came and went, and what I had thought would be a 12-hour swim was going to take a lot longer.

About 14 hours in, I rose my head and could see a small sand beach with nothing but lava rocks to the left and right. It was our only chance for a safe landing, and it appeared to be only a couple of miles away. I asked my crew the question that crews are supposed to lie about: "How much longer?" Someone said an hour. The hour came and went, and then another and another. We fought a riptide for three hours that just would not let me get nearer to the beach, though it was now so close I could make out humans.

I was becoming increasingly desperate, exhausted, and furious. Trapped in my own disappointment, thoughts, and frustrations, I was sharply torn out of my tunnel vision by a sensation comparable to a grease burn on my arm. I stopped and slapped it, only to find something like angel hair pasta was stuck on my arm and chest. As I scratched it off, it began stinging my palms and fingers. Steve told me to remain calm: This was a rare man o' war jellyfish, and I would be fine now.

About 15 minutes later came another grease burn on the opposite shoulder, followed by a violent string of German cuss words and more reassurance from Steve. Then finally, as I tilted my head to breath, a man o' war's tentacles latched onto my cheek and the inside of my mouth. I stopped and peeled tentacles off my face as my heart pounded in a bizarre limbo between panic and fury. I demanded Steve gave me a description of

50

these beasts. He explained their bodies were blue and not much larger than a quarter. I resumed swimming, and as I looked underneath me, I saw a blanket of blue dots with spaghetti tentacles floating about 4 feet below the surface as far as I could see in every direction. It appeared that only occasionally would one of them float on top, likely wounded or dead. I began to feel rage. I had not spent a fortune to travel this far, vomited harder than I ever thought possible, and shoveled through a relentless and unforgiving ocean for over 17 hours to have these little guys steal the finish from me. And with that fury came the speed to break the riptide.

As I approached the beach and unbeknownst to me, Jeff jumped in wearing a wet suit and toting his underwater camera, giving me one last solid scare for the day, as I initially mistook him for a tiger shark. The waves were as big and crushing as they had been on the opposite side of the channel, but with Jeff's help, I was able to time things just right and avoid the waves pushing me into the rocky ocean floor. Finally, an even 18 hours later, I had solid ground under my feet. And just as I walked out of the water, the Kaiwi Channel gave me a farewell present, as another wave rolling in behind me pushed me forward and knocked me off my feet. With my arms too tired to catch my fall and my mouth apparently wide open, I landed face down in the sand with a mouthful of white sand for dessert. Nice one.

Jellyfish tentacles, a swim souvenir.

My attitude was removed; gratitude and exhaustion settled in. What a team I had. For those who think this is an individual sport, you are thoroughly mistaken. These delicate attempts at making it through the sheer hostility of open water requires a team of dedicated individuals that make it all possible.

The next day, the ocean was a sheet of glass as if to mock my impatience. After a few months of licking my wounds back in Colorado, I was already searching for the next adventure, and it would be equally if not more humbling.

Chapter 9

Lessons from Cursed Waters

In ancient Germanic and Norse mythology, the concept of ancestral spirits is central. For me, the most relatable aspect of the beautiful stories about Odin and the other Norse gods is how, despite their knowledge of their respective fates, they fight their destiny relentlessly and tragically, much like humans. I hold an unusually firm belief in destiny, and the channel between Northern Ireland and Scotland, known as the North Channel, certainly made me wonder if these waters carry a family curse.

A bit of family history from my grandmother Muschka: her husband, family physician Horst Krech, was one of three sons to Captain Lieutenant Gunther Krech, a U-boat commander in World War I. (He was, therefore, my great-grandfather.). Rumor had it that Capt. Lt. Krech's father had worked for the German Emperor and embezzled money, and part of his redemption was for his sons to become professional soldiers.

Muschka and Pat, two exceptional humans.

In World War I, Capt. Lt. Krech was the commander of the UB-85, a German submarine, which wrecked on April 30, 2018. Its sailors were captured by the British, and during his interrogation, my great-grandfather spun a story that a bizarre sea monster had attacked the UB-85. Knowing the Krech side of my ancestry, tall men with sharp minds and sarcastic humor, it is easy for me to picture my great-grandfather toying with his captors. Word in the family was that he disobeyed an order to save his men and surrendered.

Capt. Lt. Krech died from pneumonia in a prisoner-of-war camp in Nottingham, England. Little did he know that two decades later two of his sons would also be prisoners of war at Nottingham: Capt. Lt. Gunther Krech II, would also be a U-boat commander, and was captured by the British following a ship wreckage. His other son, my grandfather Horst Krech was captured after he refused to abandon his patients on the front lines. Three years into their captivity, the English offered the brothers a deal: One of them would be allowed to leave, while the other would stay. Horst, often ridiculed by his brother for his warm and caring nature, sent his little brother home, spending another two years in Nottingham. The rumors about Capt. Lt. Krech II paint the picture of a man whose drive and political convictions were not shared by my grandfather, forever driving a wedge between the brothers. My grandfather Horst eventually returned home and met my Muschka, whose two young children from her first marriage were ill. These exceptional humans shared an exceptional love.

Horst, whose nickname was "Pat" (from the Latin "pater" for "father"), would die prematurely as an indirect consequence of his five years in Nottingham. According to Muschka, Nottingham conducted "Bergen-Belsen starvation drills" in an attempt to retaliate against German war crimes committed in Bergen-Belsen and other concentration camps. POWs would go without food until they were close to death, and then be fed again. For the remainder of his life, Pat was a heavyset man, towering at 6'3'' and probably close to 300 pounds. When Muschka would beg him to eat a little less for fear of his health, he would tell her "I will never be hungry again.".

Pat died at 62 from a massive stroke the very day Muschka, my mother and my uncle were to go to their annual vacation at a beautiful Italian resort. This was the only time of year he would actually close his office and eschew home visits at 3 a.m. My mother was 14, and I am not sure she ever fully recovered from losing the man who so fiercely adored his little girl. My grandmother, 48 at the time, would die in 2015 at the age of 93 – still wearing his ring and never having dated again. If I could have one wish for this lifetime, it would be to find this kind of love.

In 2016, CNN reported that the wreck of a German submarine had been discovered off the coast of Scotland by marine engineers working on an undersea power cable. Thought to be the UB -85, the sub was thought to have sustained some type of engine failure, finally debunking the almost 100-year-old myth about the ominous sea monster. Reading this, I felt a little pride in the odd humor of my great-grandfather, a professional soldier who fought a war that was more than likely not his, but just his unfortunate job.

Joe, who had witnessed my struggle with the cold in the English Channel, immediately told me signing up for the North Channel swim was a bad idea. But I was dead set on completing the "Oceans Seven," the swimming equivalent to the "Seven Summits" in mountaineering. I had three down – Catalina, England, and Molokai – and four to go – the Tsugaru Channel in Japan, the Cook Strait in New Zealand, the Strait of Gibraltar between Spain and Africa, and the North Channel. Knowing that the latter was going to be the biggest challenge, I decided to start there.

I was determined to conquer my nemesis, the cold, and spared no expense or sacrifice preparing for what would be a monumental challenge. I purchased a cattle troth and became a regular at the local gas station, buying as much ice as the trunk of my unspectacular but reliable Honda Civic would hold. I took ice baths, cold showers, swam in high altitude mountain lakes, and I even purchased an endless pool that I kept at freezing temperatures in our garage. I replaced water with weight gain shakes and milk shakes. On patrol, I constantly ate Cheetos, my favorite chips, and all my traffic tickets were a little orange on the edges from my orange Cheeto fingers. Naturally tall, lanky, and boyish looking, I was able to put on about 15 pounds. But I was still on the lighter side for a channel swimmer.

Destin and I arrived in the Northern Irish coastal town of Donaghadee and met with Captain Quinton Nelson, whose accent I could barely understand at all. Quinton immediately noted with concern that I was "a bit skinny." We had caught an exceptionally warm year and the North Channel was sitting at an all-time high of 59 degrees. The main weather obstacle would be heavy morning fog, but Quinton was hopeful that I would get a chance in the next few days.

We stayed in a beautiful little hotel on top of an Irish pub and right next to the ocean. I always had a great love for Ireland and had travelled there before with my parents. I find that no matter what part the world I find myself in, no matter how down on my luck, there is always an Irish pub. After a few treasured Luke Kelly and Dubliners songs and some cider, the world is a little less hostile again.

Swimming in the bay next to the pub, I was stung by the cold. Though my teeth and forehead were stinging, I was trying to make peace with it. And so, we waited again in a beautiful place that warmed my heart with its kind people as my body fought the cold with every training swim.

The morning we finally set off into the North Channel was foggy and surreal. It all seemed to happen too fast. Destin, Captain Nelson, his skipper, and a local volunteer were my relentless crew. In water that cold, there are two options to stay warm, both a simple matter of physics – you can either

56

eat the equivalent of a few wet suits and have your body fat insulate you, or you can try to generate some heat by swimming fast. I jumped in and had to push the pace to stay warm. The first few hours, I was quite fast, and things were close to ideal.

The North Channel has some interesting aquamarine life, including the bizarre-looking lion-mane jellyfish, whose huge orange body and long broad tentacles cause a sensation much like a paper cut. Some of them were easily 3 feet in diameter, and their tentacles were the length of my body. Oddly enough, their sting is not nearly as potent as the quarter-sized man o' war jellyfish that had given me a warm welcome to Oahu. Several hours in, things were going according to plan. Soon the fog would lift, allowing the sun to warm my back. Except it did not. Instead, a cloud cover accompanied by a cold, biting wind set in, and while I tried hard to tell my mind to focus on anything but the chill, my world was now turning into a singularity of cold and discomfort.

About 6 hours in, I could make out Scotland on the horizon, and I was determined to find its coast. I was just going to suck it up and deal with it. Ultimately, though, hypothermia takes your mind and, with it, any willpower or plan you may have had. It begins with mild disorientation, much like having a few too many drinks. It is not entirely unpleasant, as the thoughts about the cold seem to fade away into tired amusement over one's misery. Somewhere in there, I saw my entire crew on deck frantically taking pictures while I wondered where the rain was coming from. It would be a few days until I learned that a whale, easily the size of our boat, had swum up behind me and blown out some water, apparently curious at the odd little thing struggling through his ocean. It made for a treasured photo.

As I was feeding off the main boat and expecting to lose a lot of dexterity in the cold, Destin would lean overboard and hand me an open thermos cup from which to drink a protein mixture. My memory of the end of the swim is as foggy as the weather at the beginning of the swim had been. I recall trying to swim up on the big body of a lion mane jellyfish to warm up, but its slimy body slid out from underneath me, its tentacles leaving papercuts on my arms and legs. My crew was getting increasingly concerned, but Destin knew a failed swim would constitute a catastrophe for me, and he did not want to ruin the remainder of his Ireland vacation. Reminding my crew of his Special Forces emergency medical training, he talked them into letting me try this.

Another feed rolled around; it would be the last one. I only remember being furious at Destin and my crew. What mockery where they engaging in? Angrily, I yelled "Why would you put salt in my drink?" unaware I had dropped my cup in the ocean and drunk a nice cup of North Channel water. Making a last desperate attempt to get me through the four hours that were now separating me from Scotland, Quinton had me swim on the other side of his boat to shield me from the merciless wind. Unable to swim straight next to his boat, I was overcome by a feeling I never had experienced in water — and have not since. As I inhaled increasing amounts of water from the choppy waves, I started to feel panicked and was struggling to breath. I suddenly knew that I would die out here if I did not find warmth. I had stopped swimming and was gasping for air when my crew extended the ladder into the water.

As I write this 6 years later from a hot and muggy porch in Nowhere, Indiana, I remember the heartbreak as if it were yesterday. I wish I could claim that I took this well, or gracefully, or maturely. I did not. Destin helped me under deck and into my sleeping bag. I cried in pain as my femoral arteries ached and burned as the cold blood from my core made its way back to my limbs. The pain was unlike anything I have ever felt. Somehow, the boat made it back to Donaghadee, and Destin aided me into the hotel shower while the rest of the crew unloaded the boat. He left me with the advice to not use water that was too hot, and I remember thinking "What the hell? I am going to shower as warm as I damn well please!" He probably should not have left me alone. As it was, I cranked the heat and waited for the pain in my tingling body to subside.

Now, the warming-up period is the most dangerous time for an individual with hypothermia. The human body, uniquely tough and adapted for survival, will reduce circulation to the extremities to preserve crucial core heat. Warming up too quickly sends massive amounts of cold blood rushing from the extremities to the core and heart. A wave of dizziness and nausea hit me as I curled up in a ball on the shower floor clenching my aching chest. I thought of Ashton. I thought how irresponsible of a parent I was to spend two weeks so far away from him. Destin found me and put me in bed and under the down blankets, where I would remain for the next 30 hours. I was unable to sleep but finally warm – and watching the first several seasons of Game of Thrones back-to-back as the night came and went.

Destin had to convince me to leave the bed at some point, as I was crushed and infinitely disappointed in my own weakness. We quickly left

Donaghadee and traveled to Belfast and Dublin, where I drowned my sorrow at Temple Bar. I am quite certain I was an un-fun travel companion. But the neat thing about the swimming community is that we are all over the world, and we will make you feel at home if you are part of the family. An Irishman named Fergal Sommerville reached out and swam with me off the coast of Dublin, providing a much-needed return to the water and to normalcy.

Later that year, I traveled home to Germany, where I had planned a lengthwise crossing of Lake Constance, or as we call it, "Bodensee." The plan was to combine the 40-mile swim and a visit with Muschka, who had been admitted to a nursing home almost 2 years prior.

When she left her home in 2012, I made an emergency trip home as we had to clear her apartment. I could not take nearly as many things with me as I wanted to. This had been and still is the only place that was ever a home to me and seeing her leaving it just broke my heart. I spent two weeks after she entered the nursing home just sitting by her. She was still the courageous woman with a heart of gold that she always had been. I could barely stop crying. I was furious that she had been discarded to a state-run nursing home that felt so sterile. Muschka and I talked a lot, and somehow, we both knew this was goodbye.

During the visit in 2012, I was able to sneak her out of the godforsaken place, and we took a taxi to her favorite restaurant by the Rhine, a river her apartment had overlooked for more than 40 years after Pat's death. She enjoyed some beer and some good food, and the fear and disorientation vanished from her face for a few precious hours. She urged me to go home, take care of my boy and take advantage of the opportunities in America. She assured me that we would always have a special connection. I do not think there is a picture of that night in which my eyes are not watery.

My last real goodbye to Muschka, dinner near the Rhine river.

Now, in 2014, she no longer recognized me. I pushed her wheelchair through the courtyard, knowing she would love herself a hot summer day and furious that no one else would visit. As I sat on a bench, she looked at me and grinned. "You are alright. I kinda like you". I told her the same, and we peacefully sat in the sun. The nursing home had a strict policy on alcohol, but Muschka had asked me for some cognac, something I never acquired a taste for. The cognac she used to have was quite pricy and I, the cheap, open-water minimalist that I am, figured I could buy a smaller off-brand bottle and achieve the same effect. Back in her room, as I served her the cognac, the woman who liked me but was not sure who I was, immediately remarked "What cheap shit it this?". Nevertheless, she demanded a refill.

I travelled to the Alps for my swim, but the weather was not cooperating. Lake Constance borders on Austria, Switzerland and Germany, and it is a meteorological nightmare. We settled for swimming the width from Germany to Switzerland to Germany and back to Switzerland. It totaled some 22 miles, making for an OK day on the water.

A perfect picture from the swim across Lake Constance.

Back in Mannheim, I had to say a final goodbye. I will never forget Muschka sitting in the lunch area, waving courageously at me as I had to leave. Her ending up in this place while I was thousands of miles away in a country that was, and will always be to an extent, foreign to me was by far the hardest part of leaving Germany. But for me, home was never a place. It was a person — my person — and I carry her fierce strength with me every day. The way she loved me made it possible for me to love my boy the way I do. It is all good.

Chapter 10

Lessons from the Bay

Back in Colorado, I returned to patrol at the Creek and continued to work the busiest shift in town. It was as if going to a different, quieter part of town would have been admitting that I was afraid, which I was. Of course, for a cop, showing fear is not an option. I quickly learned the moment you stepped out of your car was the moment you were sized up. Being a woman posed a question mark to begin with, let alone being a woman with a funny accent. Reality is not politically correct.

I disliked the fact that we only had one officer per vehicle, which on a few occasions had gotten me into fairly serious trouble— like the time I was surrounded by an angry mob with cell phones while attempting to separate two women trying to stab each other. Driving into work at night, I would usually try to psych myself up with an energy drink, and the nightly lineup meeting helped with transitioning into a state of alert focus.

I truly despise physical fights. I am not a fighter, but I will fight to protect those in need of help or if I am sufficiently afraid. I never liked guns, and I still do not, but living out in the country alone, I keep my old patrol rifle in good shape. I still believe this country has way too many weapons circulating, but by now, it is too late to change this. And I can see the historical necessity as pioneers ventured out west on their own. It is just vastly different from Germany, where guns are rare and so are gun-related deaths.

Why would someone who dislikes guns choose a profession that has them carry one at their hip at all times? Because the humanist in me rejected the idea of the ivory tower of graduate school, and I was certain I would be unable to tolerate hearing about that little bit of depression or anxiety for which the worried well are willing to spend close to $100 an hour. I genuinely wanted to be the person that would be there on someone's worst day to ease their suffering.

I had big goals, big dreams, and a side of fantasy and privilege I had been unaware of. While my parents were not the most emotionally nurturing people in the world, I never, ever went without anything. That meant big vacations, private education, brand name clothes and a certain "we are so educated, we are better than you" attitude. Me refusing to attend the university but travelling the world doing triathlon, marrying an enlisted American soldier, and finally ending up in a profession that is not held in high regard was all likely a bit of belated teenage rebellion. Reverse psychology works wonders on this hothead.

The reality of the Creek was often disheartening — lots of property and violent crime tied in with the widespread problem of addiction. I often questioned if incarceration was just some type of graduate school for entry-level addicts who would transition from small criminal to a true life of drugs and crime. As a woman, I often would be called to take victim statements for sexual assaults and domestics, and I also became pretty decent at writing warrants. While I could barely remember how to clean my gun, the legal concepts and fine nuances of language required to get a judge to sign an arrest or search warrant at 3 a.m. came naturally to me.

Almost seamlessly, I transitioned out of patrol and was assigned to the Special Victims Section's Domestic Violence and Sex Crimes Unit as a detective. I had barely seen Destin throughout my patrol years, and our relationship was estranged and disengaged. He lived for his deployments the way any other addict lives for their rush. And so, we passed each other like two ships in the night. And just as I was finally able to work some daytime hours, I no longer had anyone to come home to. While the hours were nice, the reality was that every second week I was on call, and my phone would routinely ring in the middle of the night. That meant putting my suit on and rushing to a crime scene, hospital, or a police station.

There, I would meet my partner, a sharp and sarcastic Italian American, chronically stressed by raising three girls with his wife while working all hours of the day and night. We got along great. No small talk, no wasted time, just a shared drive for wanting to do a good investigation. We were task-oriented and hard-working. Our boss was an even more hard-working man, who had never been married and totally dedicated his life to the department. He ended up donating vacation time back to the city at the end of most years while living in the office. Leaving work on time was frowned upon, and swimming in the morning with my on-call phone at the edge of the pool in a waterproof bag, I had no reason to go home.

I was making more money than I ever had before, but instead of paying down my student loans, I bought a big house with Pike's Peak view. The house was immaculate and was only lived in on weekends with Ashton, who was now almost 11. Every other weekend was a question mark with my on-call schedule. I would let Ashton sleep at night if I got called out, but I informed the neighbors and had another detective's daughter on standby for childcare.

One night, after Ashton was in bed, I was called out around 9 p.m. to process a scene. I got the job done quickly, returning before midnight, to find a hysterical boy sitting in bed sobbing uncontrollably, holding his cell phone and covered in hives. It took him a good few minutes with me holding him before he could speak. Our house was close to a baseball stadium. There had been a game that night, followed by celebratory fireworks – that Ashton had mistaken for gun shots. He sobbed, "Mom, I thought you got shot in the hood." It was heart-wrenching.

And the job had not only taken a toll on him; it had taken a toll on me as well. My personal life consisted of swim practice and looking forward to the nights off-call to simply have a drink by myself in my perfect, unlived-in house. Patrol had shown me things I did not know existed. Death had become a more normal part of life. I had developed a robust stomach, but for some odd reason, it was fatal traffic accidents that bothered me the most. I still remember a boy Ashton's size finding his final resting place in the middle of an intersection after his mother, high on methamphetamines, had run a red light and was hit by a massive pickup truck. In times like that, I had such a desperate fury in me to be able to take a few seconds of the past back and change it. Some become cops because they like the idea of being in control, when truly having front-row seats to human tragedy is the most out-of-control thing you can imagine.

My detective salary allowed me to sign up for two big swims in 2015, a 24-mile crossing of Tampa Bay, Florida, in the spring and a 26-mile swim through Lake Memphremagog from Vermont to Quebec in the fall.

64

I was incredibly fortunate to have Joe join my crew again in Florida. The Tampa Bay Marathon swim, to my knowledge the longest actual "race" in open-water swimming, has the reputation of being a grassroots event and still has that pioneering spirit to it. Just a group full of crazies setting out into the Bay to see if they can reach the other side. I met my pilot, a Cuban living in Tampa who would have looked at home on the cover of GQ magazine, at the pasta party. We planned to meet the next morning 30 minutes before the race was to start.

Joe and I, punctual at the pier with my nutrition and equipment, had no luck in finding my captain. As the minutes passed, and we were approaching our 7 a.m. start, I finally let the race director know I was without a boat or a kayak. Thrifty me had decided to save a bit and just feed off the main boat.

As I explained my dilemma, I saw a boat on the horizon. As it came closer, I could see someone standing in the back of the boat, which appeared to be sitting awfully low on the water, using a bucket to bail water out of the boat. I learned that somehow, it had tipped over and filled with water, which caused it to move slowly and almost run out of gas. They would need more time to get rid of the water and refuel the boat, so the laid-back race director told me to "just find another swimmer to swim with."

I got lucky and found another girl who swam only a tad harder than I would have liked to start with. I made it through the first of 12 hours and was finally reunited with Mr. GQ and Joe, my quiet voice of reason and loyal friend. We settled into a rhythm. The bay was surprisingly shallow and several times, I got sand under my fingernails. We swam under numerous bridges holding multiple lanes of highway traffic afloat. I noticed a shimmering layer of oil and some type of runoff coming down the massive bridge pillars, likely exhaust fumes turned liquid polluting the Bay. If cold is my tactile nemesis, gasoline is my aromatic nemesis. When I was pregnant with Ashton, I could not even go near a gas station, and even today the pungent smell quickly gets to me. Between the exhaust fumes from my boat and whatever the ominous, rainbow-colored bridge runoff was, I was developing some pretty severe stomach issues of the second kind. Avoiding graphic detail once again, this was an extremely inconvenient situation, and all my hopes of appearing even a little bit ladylike in front of Mr. GQ were solidly down the Bay. Explaining to Joe my dilemma, I asked the boat to drive ahead a little so I could try to get things under control. But the remainder of the swim would be plagued by my food going right through me along with the Tampa Bay pollution. We made it to the beach a bit slower than planned, but I was not going to complain.

Joe and I learned that true grassroots also meant that no one had thought to organize transportation back to the start, and our captain had to run home and get to work. Joe and I found ourselves next to Tampa's party mile on the beach —him with a backpack of remaining gear and nutrition and me with a sunburn, a dirty swimsuit and the lingering feeling that I could not possibly make it through a cab ride. As we stood there, a spectator and local master swimmer approached us and kindly offered us a ride.

With no time to waste, I was back behind my desk in Colorado Springs and throwing myself into my cases before my stomach had fully recovered. Cases that revealed a darkness that transcended all education and income levels — crimes that were the stuff of dark, unspoken secrets with victims who are true survivors. I wanted nothing more than for these victims to rediscover their power, which they mistakenly believed to have been taken. Working in sex crimes meant I was honored with meaningful work.

Joe Bakel, the voice of reason on more than one swim.

Chapter 11

Lessons from the Kingdom

In the fall of 2015, I flew from Denver to Boston and made the 6-hour drive up to Newport, Vermont. Knowing little about Vermont, I was entirely amazed by its beauty. The organizer of the Kingdom Swim series, which takes place in and around Lake Memphremagog was retired prosecuting attorney Phil White. He kindly opened his "clubhouse," an add-on to his lake house that has been visited by many much more amazing open-water swimmers than me. To say Phil is a delight is an understatement. He is fiercely intelligent and eccentric, and I truly treasured our conversations, as we both had experienced our share of disenchantment with the American criminal justice system. On a few occasions, we went out for dinner, and he would suddenly go to another table and inform some unsuspecting guy that I was single and a great catch. It was flattering, but unusual.

The first night out, I met some local swimmers and the only other participant in the race, Australian sweetheart and Chicago resident, Amanda Hunt, who was Phil's girlfriend at the time. Amanda and I decided early on that we were both winners, and this is what we call each other to this day. Between Phil and Amanda, I found some much-needed laughter away from the cubicle in which I spent so much time meticulously documenting human tragedy.

The swim was entirely magical. Phil introduced me to a local legend, a woman in charge of a club solely and very seriously dedicated to finding

"Memphre," a suspected Nessie-like sea monster. This led Phil to call the swim "The Search for Memphre." Amanda and I left Newport at midnight, each of us with a small motorboat and a kayaker. Phil and a few of his friends would be somewhere out there on a pontoon party boat, which never traveled without Phil's signature pink plastic flamingo, whose name I have blasphemously forgotten.

Phil and I had tossed around the crazy idea of me doing the swim and then trying to run back to the start. My best guess is that my judgement must have been impaired at the time of our conversation, but he was prepared to let me run the 35 kilometers back from Magog, Quebec, to Newport. It was a ridiculous idea, and I abandoned it before the sun rose on the lake. The night had been cool, and as always, I was cold, which just takes a lot out of me. My fierce kayaker Gary, who would kayak 16 hours straight for me, had encouraging words and updates of when to expect sunrise. We crossed into Canada just before sunrise came.

As I swam into the morning, the water was covered with a heavy fog, and here and there were small islands in the middle of the lake. In the fog, they were reminiscent of a sea monster revealing parts of its back and lurking in the twilight. The legend of Memphre now seemed a lot more understandable. As the sun rose, a nasty and steadily annoying chop was slapping me around. The thing with waves in big oceans is that there is often a certain timing and pattern to the waves, and one can adjust to the rhythm and conserve energy by timing one's stroke just right. Lakes tend to be more prone to chop, and those little irregular waves are unpredictable and random and simply a nuisance.

Can you see Memphre lurking in the dark?

Slightly disgruntled about the chop but making steady progress, I had some visitors come by. Phil had told the police in Magog, who also cover part of the lake in a patrol boat, that we were coming, and that I was a police detective. The patrol boat escorted me for a good few hours, and the guys waved and cheered me on, making me forget about the chop and my irritation. The finish seemed drawn out, especially because I could not stop myself from looking at the pier, which, as usual, looked deceivingly close from the water, when it was still a few hours away. I crawled out onto the pier, and Phil made me one last offer to run back. I had to politely decline, because even standing was not working well.

My long work hours had not allowed for a lot of training, and the 25-mile swim had taken all I had that day. While waiting for Amanda to arrive, I fell asleep laying down on the pier right next to where I had exited the water. When she arrived, we walked around the adjacent little park that was so distinctively different from America. It was filled with French-speaking men and women, dressed in clothes I would certainly associate with Europe, having a certain chic and sophistication. It was like I was back in France, strange and beautifully different. Everywhere, there were French signs, European looking houses, men with wavy hair and scarves, and women with expensive shoes and elegant purses. I wish I could have stayed a little longer, but I quickly found myself back in Colorado, and I was in for a few months unlike anything I had ever experienced.

I was struggling to stay on top of my large case load of sexual assaults and felony domestic violence cases, and my evenings and weekends without Ashton were now solidly spent working. I made an attempt at dating and soon was seeing a patrol sergeant I had never worked with, but who was a former detective and understanding of my schedule. I had never dated another cop, but with us having never worked together, it seemed like a possibility.

Halloween 2015 was a Saturday, a morning I usually spent in my cubicle trying to get caught up. I heard the deputy chief yelling on the phone about some type of active-shooter situation in downtown Colorado Springs with several victims. Around me, on-call phones went off, and detectives flooded into the station. I had never responded to a homicide callout, but this was an all-hands-on-deck situation.

When I arrived on scene, the street was blocked off, and the body of a young man was laying face down on top of his bicycle, where he had been executed. He was wearing red Vans, a memory that has always followed me.

My diligent sergeant was busy assigning tasks to detectives. Apparently, the shooter, also a young man, had walked out of his home carrying a rifle. Walking down the street, he first encountered a father and veteran riding his bicycle — the first victim I saw. He then passed a halfway house, where two women on a front porch had been unable to escape in time. The shooter had been walking towards a school that was holding a large sporting event when our officers got into a firefight with him. The shooter was the fourth life tragically lost that day. It felt a little as if my sergeant and the rest of the exclusively male homicide detectives wanted me out of their important business, so I was told to talk to the deceased suspect's girlfriend, whose house was directly across from the red Vans I could not stop staring at. They seemed to say that this was just a young dad, a guy like you and me, who had left his home that day, not suspecting he would never return.

And so, I was welcomed into a young woman's home along with a victim advocate to help support her. She was just a little younger than me, her home comfortable and clean, a sharp-minded woman with whom I would have loved to be friends with, in a parallel universe. Somehow, no one had told her that her boyfriend, who had lived across the street from her (where the body of the young father was still laying) had been shot and killed by police.

I always found the moment another human realized they had lost a loved one to be one of the most awful things to see. But somehow, this exceptional woman calmed herself, and we talked for hours.

I learned that her boyfriend had periodically struggled with bipolar disorder and as is common, had gotten off his medication — likely missing the delightful feeling of mania and tired of the side effects of the medication. However, he had grown increasingly agitated and paranoid, and having isolated himself, his mind had spun theories of an impending police state, making him more and more afraid. His family had gotten concerned about his odd statements on the phone, and his brother, an attorney, was on an airplane to get him help the very moment the tragedy unfolded. Her boyfriend had spoken to no one besides her in months, and it was left to her to provide all the answers to a town that demanded them to ease the spreading fear.

Later that evening, while cancelling yet another date, the patrol sergeant decided to end our brief relationship, but I was too tired to care. Finally, off-call, I sat in my oversized, lifeless house with my large African pet tortoise, drinking raspberry vodka from the bottle, my heart and mind spinning. But life went on, as it always does.

A little more than two weeks later, I suddenly awoke at 3 in the morning to a single thought, surprisingly in English: "And then she was gone." I knew immediately. I could *feel* it. I quietly got up, drove to the pool, and swam. When I returned to my car, I had several missed calls from my mother. Muschka had passed away on Nov. 18, 2015, at the age of 93. It had been time for her suffering to end. In 2012, when Muschka was still lucid, she told me I should not travel to her funeral when the time came, that it was not for her but for the family to make themselves feel better after visiting not nearly enough. Worrying over my ability to control my impulsivity, I decided to not travel home for the funeral on Nov. 27.

Instead, on that very day, I was again trying to catch up with my caseload, when another tragedy unfolded with unstoppable vengeance, forcing me into a state of reactive terror. The detectives gathered in a briefing room and learned an active shooter had opened fire at a local Planned Parenthood clinic, likely a religious extremist violently protesting the birth control and abortions the clinic provided. Listening to the radio traffic and unable to do anything, I felt suffocatingly helpless. And then came the radio transmission that an officer was laying behind a dumpster where he had sought cover. Checking the roster of cars working that afternoon, I realized I had way too many friends out there. SWAT teams evacuated a nearby shopping center, and after a 6-hour standoff that claimed the lives of two civilians and one officer and wounded over a dozen others, SWAT freed those trapped inside the Planned Parenthood facility and brought them to the nearby evacuation site where I was among the ones conducting interviews. I remember a remarkable physician, whose concern was completely focused on his patients, being a calming presence. I took statements of terrified humans that hid under desks and behind barricaded doors, where they survived the endless ordeal. Now in custody, the suspect confirmed he had a delusional obsession about needing to stop Planned Parenthood from their mission.

Shortly thereafter came the surreal police funeral of Officer Garret Swasey, who was actually an officer at a nearby college campus who had come to help. Our commander forgot the at-ease command, and so we stood saluting for a long time until the vehicles carrying his family members arrived. I would have not dared to lower my arm.

His widow, a gorgeous woman, and a little elementary-school-aged boy and girl followed the flag-covered cascade. She gave a speech of hope and gratitude that seemed to be fueled by an out-of-this world strength. That night, there was more raspberry vodka in my ghost house. And again, life went on.

I began having lots of difficulty sleeping and went to our health clinic. They suggested I take an anti-depressant, which I did. The better suggestion would have been to not work 60 hours or more a week, but they knew better than to bring it up.

One night, during another call to the hospital, I spoke to a young girl who reported a man with a green mask and a gun had come to her hotel room and sexually assaulted her. She seemed to be hiding something, and we suspected that she had been working at the hotel. The whole story sounded a bit too much like the boogey man. Nevertheless, we processed the scene and did our best. I had long forgotten about the call when my tirelessly focused sergeant called me in his office and shared there had been a very similar report of a rape in the Denver area: a prostitute, a green mask, a gun. I rushed the lab to process all the prints we had from the room, and one perfect fingerprint from a condom wrapper later, we had an identity: an Air Force soldier whose prints were in the database because he had recently obtained a concealed-carry permit. With his phone records, I was able to place him at both scenes and obtain an arrest warrant. His chain of command

72

pretended to call him in for a random drug test. When he walked into the room, his eyes met my badge and then, my eyes. He did not speak. He knew.

We searched his home and his vehicle, where we found a large external hard drive in his trunk. It was late in the afternoon, and I was going to try to go home on time for a date with a bright-eyed Fort Carson soldier who had been sending me endearing little messages in German for a few days. Our computer expert came into my cubicle and told me he had an entire hard drive of what appeared to be recordings of rapes I needed to see. I laughed at him, telling him that was a good one and to have a great night. Only it was no joke.

What ensued was weeks and weeks of watching hundreds of hours of footage I would truly like to delete from the hard drive in my mind. My partner and I went to most of the shady hotels in town, trying to recognize rooms we saw in the sexual assault videos and looking at guest records. The bond for the suspect was now in the millions, announced with a shaking upper lip by the petite, female judge. Ultimately, two victims in Colorado Springs and one in Denver were willing to work with us. The suspect, in his early 30s, pled guilty and accepted a deal of 30 years on an indeterminate sentence, which meant he would have to pass a psychosexual evaluation to ever be free again.

I was burnt out and tired, and I found some comfort in the arms of the Fort Carson soldier with the bright blue-green eyes who instantaneously had my heart. Much like when I ended my triathlon career 13 years prior, I wanted out and away, and it was my wild and fantasy-prone heart and mind that jumped head over heels into reckless love, desperately hoping it would be my last one.

Chapter 12

Lessons from the Great Lakes

The man with the bright blue-green eyes, at close to 24 years of military service, was nearing his retirement. I vividly remember our first date; it was a fairy tale. I had been on a remarkable number of online-initiated blind dates during my off-call weeks, but there was never once a spark of chemistry. I am picky and intense; dating is not my strong suit.

I saw him standing there in the front of the restaurant and immediately thought to myself that someone must have been incredibly stupid to have divorced him. On the way to our table, he grabbed my hand and said, "Look, it fits perfectly in mine!" The lonely detective was in love, and quite frankly, I would have married him right then and there. He went on to talk about his divorce, and a heavy sadness surrounded him as he shared that his two children were living in another state, and he rarely saw them. I saw this sadness as the ability to care and love deeply. It did not hurt that he had been stationed near my hometown, drove a Mercedes with some German CDs in the player and spoke a little German.

Sure, there were little red flags as early as three weeks in: his dating account remaining active, or his flying out of town for a weekend for supposed military training while actually visiting a woman. My profession did little to instill faith in humanity or love, so I must admit to snooping around a little (or a lot) throughout our time together. Really, it was a setup for failure: finding things felt awful and made we wonder if it should even be discussed; not finding something somehow made me feel like I was an investigative failure and acting ridiculous. I had never been very jealous in previous relationships, but I guess my intuition was just sensing the reality that I was nevertheless determined to deny.

He wanted to retire to his small, rural hometown in Indiana, and I liked the idea of us ending our violent careers and retreating into the country to find peace and love and that elusive home I was continuing to look for. He would always say he married me out of compromise, since I gave up my life in Colorado to move with him. That statement more than likely foreshadowed our marriage (his fourth and my third) were doomed in more than just statistical ways already. But when the current works against you, you swim harder. I was determined to find a home in him and decided to give it my all.

I sold the unlived-in house with the great view and moved into the downtown home he had fixed up to be quite lovely. One night, when I was asked to go on another evening call during my off-call week, I did something detectives do not do —at least none of the ones I have heard of. Not willing to miss yet another evening with the man I was so intrigued by, I gave my hard-working sergeant my two weeks' notice. I had not planned on it that day: I had tossed the idea around for some time, but not until I was going to have a smooth transition with another job already waiting. I guess in some ways it was a long time coming.

I found work transitionally as a psychotherapist at the local community health center in Colorado Springs while waiting for my intended to retire and for us to start our new life somewhere where no one knew me as a cop, where no one wanted to retaliate against me. Somewhere I would find peace and a home. I had crafted a beautiful fairy tale in my restlessly driven, never-tiring, hardly sleeping, limitlessly fantasy-prone mind.

I am sure any reader must see the problem with all this from a mile away, as it is glaringly obvious. Not only was I actively denying problematic facts such as finding out he and the older neighbor lady across the street were unlikely friends with benefits or continuing to find messages of him trying to meet other women. We both had a lot of stuff going on. My job had wounded my ability to trust about as much as the dark sneaking around of his Special Forces career had wounded his ability to be honest. What a perfect storm. We married in his living room about 10 months after we met with only our kids present — pragmatically, somewhat unromantically and cost-efficiently, but I adored the idea of him.

And once again, Katie set off into the sunset, leaving her home in the Rockies behind to venture into the unknown. Our arrival in Indiana was riddled with stressors. I sorely missed my paychecks and tried to make some money by selling swim-training plans and doing some coaching at the local YMCA. We bought a fixer-upper home on the extremely cheap, and it turned into a nightmare. We had romanticized about tiny and simple living but once we had three prepubescent children with us over the summer, tiny living was suddenly the worst possible thing on Earth, and our small home not enough space for sanity. Reality was knocking on our door hard.

The man with the bright eyes and I shared a lot of characteristics: passion, intensity, and an unlimited mind. Unlimited minds are rare these days. Most people are limited by what they can think and dream of as possible, and few can go to the absolute limit of what the human body and mind can do. We shared the ability to do so. The distinct problem with this is that an element of grounding, reason and calm needs to be present to stop the perfect storm from becoming a perfect hurricane.

My heart has always had a loyalty that makes sense to very few people. It is not for moral or religious reasons; rather, I lack the capability to talk to a man that I like and simultaneously talk to another. My heart is a one-way player. Just as I am uncapable of meaningless encounters, so was he uncapable of the prison he considered monogamy and marriage to be. Leaving all judgement aside, these are simply different ways of being in the world, but they cannot be together well.

It only took about a year, and many violent disturbances, to realize the fairy tale had come to a screeching halt and was rapidly turning into a mockery of the detective's dream of love and peace. I cannot say I was entirely the victim. An unpleasant raspberry vodka habit did not aid my demeanor and would bring out harsh and hurtful words about his infidelity, triggering his anger. The dynamics were toxic really: no one innocent, but both of us wounded by the violent things we had encountered. I have always been fiercely outspoken about my trauma, (about everything really), though I think the most fitting description would be "blunt"— not meant to wound but out of intense emotion, passion, and impulsivity.

I feel like the moment I lose my ability to be genuine will be the moment my dark passenger will return. I am forced by fear into merciless honesty. As I am writing this, at age 41, I find such beautiful relief in my choice to be real. Not that I deserve the comparison to or will ever understand the suffering of Dr. Viktor Frankl, aforementioned Holocaust survivor and author of the unfathomable book *Mans's Search for Meaning*, but as he does in the book, I've realized no matter what occurs around me, I have the marvelous freedom to be a real, vulnerable, imperfect human who does what she genuinely believes in. Being cool, popular, liked or whatever I was supposed to be as a teenager has finally become irrelevant. There is no more room for ego — only room for immersion into life and, hopefully, the experience of another human to make his or her life more meaningful.

I halted my swimming for the man with the bright eyes in 2016, but I was incapable of sustaining this change and did another Swim Around Key West in 2017. I returned to a very disgruntled husband, who had four days with three kids to himself and was angry. I tried a triathlon comeback in the fall of 2017 with a Half-Ironman in Los Cabos, Mexico, combining it with our belated honeymoon. It was all overshadowed by his anger of what he called my "obsession" and my anger of him being the center of female attention at the pool bar. He was endlessly cool, with endless Special Forces stories, while I felt redundant and lonely.

Our marriage was not well. He missed his deployments, and I could feel how my expectations of a peaceful life and fidelity were making him feel caged — like I had taken his life away from him, like he had been reduced to the insignificance and unsexiness of daily life. He said that he envied me for having swimming, while he felt he did not have anything challenging left to do. I would tell him to enjoy the peace of not having anything left to prove, but my restless soul could wholeheartedly relate to the fear of stagnation and of becoming insignificant.

He never spoke of what happened during his numerous deployments to the Middle East, Africa, and Europe. His culture, with its code of hypermasculinity, did not allow vulnerability. It is not by chance that 22 American soldiers die every single day by suicide — more than any recent war casualties — yet it is not mentioned much. This silent suicide epidemic is so close to the topic I had studied in so much detail in graduate school, but he did not need help — he just needed me to stop asking questions.

Finally, tired of the fixer-upper, where every time something else broke, another bill would roll our way, I urged him to sell the home. We found a fierce realtor who also happened to be a Colorado State graduate. In the fixer-upper, we had slept upstairs but there was no bedroom door. And even though I am European and not overly modest (while checking in for my first Ironman Hawaii, I was specifically told I could not simply get naked and change in the transition area without getting disqualified, a speech reserved for the European athletes), and generally consider the unclothed human body a normal thing, having three children and no bedroom door was not enough privacy for my taste.

The realtor found a beautiful country home with a community pond that allowed swimming that fit our budget. But more importantly, she kept teasing me, it had a bedroom door. And even more importantly, we got out from underneath the fixer-upper from hell without losses. It was supposed to be another new start, and I was excited to move in. It was the fall of 2018.

I finally found a permanent place of employment at the local community mental health center as a psychotherapist. Once again, I was actually making adult-sized pay checks, which was a relief given the shakiness of our nuptials. Plus, it fed my deep love for community mental health. I serve primarily clients who live below the poverty line, many battling addiction, and other dark passengers. I have such respect for my clients' strength, many of them not as privileged as myself. They are fantastic humans who need genuine care and treatment, not merely incarceration. I work for a wonderful organization that truly makes an impact on those who need it the most. I am once again honored with meaningful work.

About that time, I thought I should return to marathon swimming to get a bit of myself and a bit of balance back. It would allow me to not be so tunnel-visioned on the relationship and give him more space. I signed up for a 24-mile crossing of Lake Erie in the summer of 2019 and began structured training again. I was swimming every day already, but not in an intentional and focused manner. I was excited and felt myself again, having both a career and swimming goals. Ashton had also done a terrific job with the transition. Since our move, he had discovered a deep passion for music and was participating in choir, musicals, piano, and guitar lessons, while also finding a wonderful mentor in a music teacher at the local high school.

As the swim approached, there was a lot of back-and-forth as to whether my husband would or would not be on my crew, meaning the remaining crew, all from Erie, Pennsylvania, had to scramble for emergency backups. But as he was in a good mood the weekend of the swim, he drove me the 5 hours to the small lake town, where we met my fierce crew for dinner. I was tingly with joy and excited to be back. We had a great dinner and I learned about my crew: Rob, who had just done the swim the year prior and would kayak; Drew, a triathlete who would kayak as well, as well as captain Mike Green and his wife, Sue. I was back in my element, feeling fully alive, with people who shared my passion for the water. It was beautiful, and I hardly noticed that my husband spoke little. No one had asked much about his unquestionably exceptional military career, and he soon relayed that he was bored of swim talk. The night flew by with little sleep for me (as usual), and we reunited with the crew at 5 a.m. at the pier in Erie.

The two hours travelling from Erie to Canada while watching the sunrise were truly magical. I had forgotten how much I live for these moments, how they carry my life by enriching it with meaning and making me feel a part of beautiful nature. Just a few layers of sunscreen, and I was off the boat to briefly touch Canadian soil. My soul was elated to be back.

My two kayakers, Drew, and Rob, both calming presences sharing my love for the sport, set off into the sunrise with me. It took me a long time to settle into a rhythm. The water was in the low 70s, so cold was only a minor factor. But I still complained about some of the cold pockets, being thinner than I had been a few years prior. I told my crew it was not unusual for me to take several hours to get comfortable, but obviously any complaint of cold or feeling stiff early on was to be taken seriously.

Rob and Drew providing guidance and my feeds on Lake Erie.

We were off to a pace that would have broken the women's record sitting at roughly 13 hours, and the wind was pushing me back to America. Josh, the diligent organizer of the swim, kept a close eye on my progress, and was always a few steps ahead, considering everything and anything that could go wrong. I am quite sure I added considerably to his stress level when he learned how little I had trained. I had maxed out for Lake Erie at around 30 kilometers a week, the same distance I had maxed out at for the English Channel or Molokai, which would be considered a low training volume, roughly half of most other channel swimmers. I added more stress when, days before the swim, my spouse was a question mark for the crew — and still more stress when I said I was cold about 2 hours in. But that stress simply reflected how terrific a job he does keeping swimmers safe, thus ensuring the future of the swim itself.

After 3 hours, I finally loosened up and was able to enjoy the infinite lake around me. To me, the moment you can no longer see the shore on either side of you is sacred and special, something few people have experienced, especially having swum to that point out of their own strength. It is like somehow having a special permission to be in outer space, a briefly tolerated guest that has only arrived there with a massive logistical and highly specialized effort. A guest out of its natural habitat but determined to make do.

About 7 hours in, I began having some pain in my left shoulder, which being a right-side breather for 30 years, is not uncommon for me. I was able to switch to bilateral breathing but was beginning to lose a little speed. At the same time, my "favorite" companion, the nasty little chop, made an appearance to ensure my ego would remain in check, and I would be sufficiently humbled by the Great Lakes.

While it was annoying and forced us off our record pace, I was simply happy to be there and to have my husband there, although he looked miserable. He had agreed to kayak the last half hour to the finish with me but somehow had gotten in too soon, around 3 miles out. I felt some anxiety building knowing how disgruntled he would be and knowing I was down to an unsexy and inglorious, but steadily moving, 2 miles per hour.

The finish at Lake Erie was unlike anything I have ever experienced. Several boats began to escort me on the way to the shore, where I saw spotlights and what appeared to be some type of a crowd on the beach. The sun was setting, and I was thinking how a day spent on the water is just the most perfect of days. My heart full, I stumbled out of the water to give the event director Josh Heynes a hug while a crowd of maybe 100 people clapped. There were a few news cameras, and I answered some questions about my "why" — how swimming to me feels like flying, and how grateful

I was to be there. I must admit, I kind of wished I would have looked a little less waterlogged and more ladylike, but it didn't seem to be in the cards for me. I was still wild Katie, who could not seem to sit still long enough to not ruin her hair.

Unprecedented levels of attention at Lake Erie.

My spouse was very unhappy. The kayak had been uncomfortable, and he was quite annoyed by all the ruckus around me. The next day, on our way back to rural Indiana, the mood was a little tense, but my heart was too full to really notice. We returned home, to our daily routines and what I thought would be our life, when it really was the calm before yet another storm. Muschka's saying keeps coming back to me: "First, it will be different. Second, it will be different from what you thought it was going to be like." And so, it was.

Chapter 13

Lessons from the Little Pond

Being back in my element also meant I was back to looking for new challenges. I had pressed the pause button on my personal aspirations to focus on and obsess over the man with the bright eyes. With him alternating between complaining that I was not home enough and complaining that I was suffocating him, it seemed like focusing on something outside of us would be good, especially as "us" had become such a challenging place.

The week I swam Lake Erie was also the week I returned to school, pursuing a Ph.D. in performance psychology, online from Grand Canyon University out of Phoenix. Unfinished business just does not sit well with me. It remains unclear if this degree will ever pay for itself, as is not clinical in nature and, therefore, does not add to my credentials as a psychotherapist. But it has my heart. Just as much as I enjoyed graduate school at Colorado State, I thoroughly love being back to expanding my mind. There are few things more invigorating than tossing ideas around and broadening one's knowledge and horizon. I hope that one day, I can find a university teaching position allowing me to write and research more.

I also desperately want to find the next challenge in the water, and I have long harbored a secret dream to break the 24-hour-mark of continuous swimming. Watching Sarah Thomas set world records, including swimming for close to 60 hours straight, brought back my own desire to explore my personal limits. Even though I am 41 years old, I believe I have not discovered them yet. I always did better, the longer the event, except for this thing called marriage, but I am not planning to leave that chapter unfinished either.

My readers might wonder: why swim so far? What is out there in the vast nothingness of the open water? Something happens in my body right around the 10-hour mark. Actually, it happens in my restless mind. It is finally quiet, immersed in the experience of just swimming. I let go of conscious thought in a meditative state that I can only otherwise accomplish through raspberry vodka — and that is more of a numbness than an immersion in the world and nature itself. I feel guilty saying this, but some of my best moments in my life have been in relative solitude out in the ocean. Others have been spent with my Muschka and with my boy, who might quite possibly have raised *me* and is growing into the most beautiful kind soul I could have ever imagined.

So, in my quest for the next swim, I tried to find warm water and someone who would accommodate a 40-50-mile swim. I found that person in Suz Dyson. She was wholeheartedly supportive of me attempting a fortysomething-mile double crossing of the St. Lucia Channel — from St. Lucia to Martinique and back — in the beautiful, endless, turquoise Caribbean Sea.

My husband was not pleased. "When will you stop?" he demanded. "When will it be enough?" I didn't know, but I can love, nevertheless. And I can love hard, with the best of them. Yet he said I had "caged the eagle," and that he was absolutely miserable. In March 2020 after an argument, he literally ran from what I thought was our home, never to return. Just like that.

He left just as COVID-19 hit, and with it came breathtaking uncertainty. "Please come home," my mind begged him. No such luck. Just as my highs are more intense than most people's, so are my lows. Several weeks of sleeping on the living room couch, afraid of the bed that once was ours, and a blurry bender of cheap vodka later, I told my work I was not well and needed help. They were wonderful and supportive and provided additional supervision when I told them I knew I needed to climb out of the bottle of vodka so cheap, it could probably power my riding lawn mower. Yes, there had been violence and infidelity in my marriage, but I felt so very, very small. How would anyone ever love me if the man with the bright eyes, who had meant so much to me, could not? I have no idea whose fault it all was, and it no longer matters.

After he filed for divorce, it was just my boy, my two beautiful dogs, Freya and Isa, my two tortoises, Louis and Flea, and me in the beautiful country home I had refinanced in my name. Thank heaven the governor of Indiana authorized psychotherapy services by phone, meaning I could work from home.

I eventually got back off the couch, feeling raw and wounded and angry. I posted way too much on social media, again feeling that if I were not all honest, raw, and genuine, either the old dark passenger or its shapeshifting best friend, raspberry vodka, would catch up with me. So many dreams, so much life I hoped for, was gone in an instant, with no closure, in the middle of an unprecedented pandemic.

But even on my couch, where I slept in a puddle of cheap vodka, there were still people who reached out to me — cops I used to work with who knew this dark place and my open-water swimming family. South African swimmer and fellow adventurous soul, Ryan Stramrood, whom I've never met in real life, became a light in the darkness, sending words of wisdom and encouragement from some 20-plus flight hours away. The open-water swimming family is grand, transcending continents with ease. We get each other. Those who have been in the middle of the ocean, with nothing but water in all directions, afraid of what lurks in the depth while dealing with whatever is stinging us on the surface, are automatically family.

The St. Lucia Double Channel attempt was pushed from June 2020 to October and, as I am writing this, the world is still in an unknown, unprecedented situation. Who would have thought the new decade would start this way, with lockdowns and people wearing masks and violent demonstrations for racial equality?

But Muschka, my Muschka, was 17 years old when a war started that she was too young to comprehend, if it was even comprehensible at all. Her parents had married her off to a 45-year-old BASF chemist, and as the war began to erupt in 1937, she was 20, with two infants and a husband who had locked himself into his laboratory. (Though he was brilliant, he was also suffering from schizophrenia. Rumor has it he spent most of the war believing he was a mouse.) But Muschka figured it out, and so can I. Life is malleable and imperfect and always so different from our sweet plans. But I think of Muschka and the grace that surrounded her. She was the soul of the 16-unit apartment building she lived in for over 40 years after Pat's premature death.

As a triple divorcee, living alone with my amazing son and animals in the middle of Nowhere, Indiana, and training daily in the 250-yard-long pond behind my house, I am trying to write the next chapter. The pond is warm and shallow. It's a bit muggy and smells like fish, and I have never, ever seen anyone else swim in it. The water is murky, dark, and coarse — a bit like the past few months. My biggest fear in the little pond are the large catfish that fishers catch and release, often leaving a large, bloated, and ungodly smelling cadaver floating on the water. I diligently scan the water surface for these floaters, as my worst nightmare would be swimming into one of them. I have termed this "catfishexplodiophobia."

Swimming has been the sole constant in my life, and water has been the very closest that I have had to a home. It has taught me peace, humility, dedication, discipline, passion, and patience. You may have heard the story of Randy Pausch, a professor of computer science, human-computer interaction, and virtual design at Carnegie Mellon University in Pittsburgh. He prepared what he called "the last lecture" to students and family after learning he had cancer and only months left to live. In that lecture, he spoke of sports as being a "head-fake" for real life. Swimming has been exactly that for me. I never made the Olympics; I never became famous or important or fast. But the water has taught me so very many lessons. I learned how to persevere in the face of adversity. I learned work ethic, discipline, persistence in the face of failure and, as a bonus, travelled the world.

Today, as I venture out for my daily training swims in the dirty little pond behind the house, I feel infinitely grateful. No matter what country I am in, no matter how lost in the world, no matter how great or shattered I feel, my water is there. I can jump into it and, stroke by stroke, settle into a weightless rhythm. If I do not swim for a time, I quickly begin having vivid dreams about swimming, though in my dreams I swim in air, overlooking houses and the rest of the world as my strokes push the air away, enabling me to fly.

Somewhere in Nowhere, Indiana.

I do not know what chapter 14 will bring. I hope it brings an exceptionally long swim, but so much more importantly, I hope it brings Ashton a life of genuineness, contentment, and peace. And as far as I am concerned – as long as there is a breath in me and water to swim in – I will never, ever give up on finding the kind of love Muschka and Pat had.

I am doing well academically and in my career. I have a nice place to stay, my beautiful tiny zoo and a young man who makes me so immensely proud. I do get upset that love, the thing I want most other than seeing Ashton thrive has not been in my cards. The detective has remained lonely, still dreams of the red Vans, and is terrified by the lions sleeping among us and the terrible dark secrets that lurk hidden under facades of normalcy.

I am not sure where to go next. Ashton will finish high school here in Indiana in another three years, and we are both wanting to venture out after that. But then what? My plans of companionship and a peaceful future here in the middle of nowhere have evaporated, so I've again signed on some dating sites. I am working hard on my dissertation about how autonomy support aids athletes in the development of healthy and adaptive motivation. My topic choice was likely impacted by my experience of not having a say in my early athletic career and burning out so very quickly and with such devastating consequences.

My pets are the heart of this house, and my boy, the pride of my soul. Life is good, but I wonder what Muschka would tell me to do now. I have been isolating myself out here in the country. I love the quiet, especially the lack of traffic – driving has never been the same for me after the horrid accidents I have seen. For that matter, humanity has never been the same after knowing how the wolves sleep among us. While I am often deeply alienated and lonely, I am also oddly content and more at peace with myself than ever before.

Yet I know Muschka would not allow me to soak in self-pity. We all must continuously reinvent ourselves. Remember the humanist Jewish professor from Colorado State? He used to tell me how much he loves painting rooms, because once he is done, the task is finished and utterly completed. Our human existence does not work that way. We are ever imperfect, ever reinventing ourselves, ever searching for meaning and love for the duration of our existence.

My water has taught me so much, and I believe that anytime we get close to mastering anything, the process of thriving and the activity itself begins to mimic the nature of life.

My water taught me perseverance in the face of failure. And fail we will, over and over again.

My water has taught me how to be intrinsically motivated. I no longer care about what anyone else or some record books say.

My water has kept me grounded. I swim on the best and the worst of days even the days when my heart feels so raw it makes my muscles ache.

I often feel like I am 250 years old: so much life lived, places visited, challenges accepted, failures overcome, and memories made. I desire peace and crave a home. Most of all I want the elusive "real love" I know exists. But such is the human condition: ever-seeking, ever-craving, ever-wanting. I am still hoping to find a home outside of the water, but I am incredibly blessed to have the kind of a home I can return to anywhere in this world. Perhaps my true home is in the water, swimming back out into the open and the unknown, eagerly awaiting what the tides have in store for me. This end is only the beginning.

A brief glimpse ahead.

ISBN-13: 9798674807315

Feedback, Questions, Comments?
Contact: kathrinblair@gmail.com